ABRAHAM
The Friend of God

OTHER BIBLICAL CHARACTER STUDIES BY WALTER C. KAISER, JR.
The Lives and Ministries of ELIJAH and ELISHA
ABRAHAM The Friend of God

Coming Soon

DAVID A Man After God's Own Heart

MOSES The Man Who Saw the Invisible God

JOSEPH From Prison to Palace

JOSHUA A True Servant Leader

NEHEMIAH The Wall Builder

SOLOMON The King with a Listening Heart

THE TWELVE The "Minor" Prophets Speak Today

JACOB The Journey from Jacob to Israel

ZECHARIAH The Quintessence of Old Testament Prophecy

DANIEL The Handwriting is on the Wall

RUTH The Moabite and the Providence of God

ESTHER God Preserves the Jewish Nation

ABRAHAM
The Friend of God

Walter C. Kaiser, Jr.

Lederer Books
an imprint of
Messianic Jewish Publishers
Clarksville, MD 21029

Cover Design by Lisa Rubin,
Messianic Jewish Publishers
Graphic Design by Yvonne Vermillion,
MagicGraphix.com
George Koch, Editor

1   2021
ISBN 9781951833077

Published by:
Lederer Books
An imprint of
Messianic Jewish Publishers
6120 Day Long Lane
Clarksville, MD 21029

Distributed by:
Messianic Jewish Publishers & Resources
Order line: (800) 410-7367
lederer@messianicjewish.net
www.MessianicJewish.net

Dedication

To my sons for their continued walk with their Lord:

Walter Christian III
Brian Addison
Jonathan Kevin

1 Corinthians 2:9

Table of Contents

Preface

Abraham: The Friend of God and the Mirror of "The Gospel of God"[1]

Abraham is referred to in Scripture as the "Father of many nations." In fact, the Ishmaelites, the Edomites, the offspring of Keturah, and all the Israelites come from him! There are two other nations—the Moabites and Ammonites—that come from his nephew Lot, a man whose life and times were closely related to those of Abraham. This makes Abraham something of a unique character, for even though Abraham takes a most central position in the book of Genesis, he is not the ancestor of just one single national group. As a consequence, most of the story about Abraham must be gathered from a number of stories in this book of Genesis instead of a single "Abrahamic source."

This means there are only four sections of material in Genesis that could act as real Abrahamic sources: (1) The initiation of the promise (12:1–9); (2) the Covenant Sacrifice (15:1–21); (3) the Covenant of Circumcision (17:1–27) and (4) the Vindication of the Ancient Promise (22:1–19).

The material that covers the life and work of Abraham emphasizes the Covenant between God and Abraham and the most significant part of that document, the promise of a son and heir of all Abram has been blessed with. It is this emphasis that makes its resemblance to the gospel in the New Testament so special and noteworthy!

The Promise of the Birth of a Son

The Promise-Plan in the Abrahamic Covenant of Genesis 12, 15, 17 and 22 focuses on the birth of a son named Isaac. In that regard, this portion of Genesis is similar to the New Testament, which declares that the promises of God can only come through the birth of his Son (John 1:14, 18; Romans 8:3). Everything depends on whether this son will be born to Abraham, and so everything in the Gospel depends on the birth of the Son of God!

The Promise of a Miraculous Birth

But in both narratives found in the Abrahamic story and the Christmas story, the son that is to be born will be borne by the miracle of God! Mary gave birth to Yeshua as a virgin, but the Bible goes to great lengths to show that Sarah's birth of Isaac was likewise a supernatural event! Without the birth of this Son there would be no story to tell!

The Promise Is Made by God Alone

It is important to note that the Lord God moved as a flaming torch between the cut pieces of the animals in Genesis 15 when the Covenant was made. And the New Covenant was made by the Lord alone with the house of Israel and the house of Judah in Jeremiah 31:31–34.

The Promise Has a Sign That Goes With It

The sign of the Covenant for Abraham and the Old Testament was the sign of circumcision (Genesis 17:11), which, like baptism, is a similar sign in God's new community of believers. Likewise, the bread of the Lord's Supper symbolizes his broken body for all who believe as the cup symbolizes his blood spilt on our behalf.

The Promise of Being Aliens and Sojourners

God called Abraham in Genesis 12 to leave his homeland in Haran (after he had previously left Ur of the Chaldees with his father Terah, who stopped and later died in Haran) and to take up journeying as a pilgrim with God away from his homeland. In the New Testament the believer is taught that one's citizenship is in heaven; therefore, we are not to love the world or its culture, much as Abraham was taught to hold lightly his earthly citizenship.

The Promise of the Death of His Son

One of the most difficult commands in the Bible to grasp is the call God gave to Abraham to sacrifice his only son. That son was at the very heart of the covenant promises. However, God provided in the nick of time an animal substitute that had gotten caught by its horns in the bushes. And God's own Son goes to the cross to die for the sins of the world. Yes, the sacrifice of Isaac was a "test," but in Yeshua's death it was a climactic moment in bringing eternal life to all who believe in the Man of Promise!

The Promise of the Resurrection of the Son

To be sure, Isaac was not ultimately killed by the uplifted knife of Abraham, for God directly and suddenly intervened at the last moment to break the sentence of death that hung over Isaac's head. But the Lord's dramatic intervention and his provision of a substitute became an earnest of how God's sending his only Son to be a substitute would function for all our sin as well. What a glorious gospel and what a magnificent provider through a Promise-Plan that began several millennia before the actual fulfillment became a living reality in Jerusalem centuries later.

No wonder this man Abraham is called the "Friend of God." In him and in his life is depicted so much of what God had planned to accomplish so that all men and women might be set free.

Abraham and God's Covenant With Him: The Promised Plan for Israel and the Nations – 11:27–25:11

Terah took his son Abram, his grandson Lot, son of Haran, and his daughter-in-law Sarai, the wife of his son Abram, and together they set out from Ur of the Chaldeans to go to Canaan. . . . They settled there [in Haran]. . . . And [Terah] died in Haran (Genesis 11:31–32).

Introduction

The study of Genesis often begins by dividing the book into two unequal parts: 1:1–11:26 and 11:27–50:26. Both parts are thought to have five sections, beginning with the phrase, "These are the generations of," or something of that sort. The first section of the book, then, is called "Primeval History," with the introductory phrase containing the Hebrew word *toledoth*, appearing in Genesis 2:4, 5:1, 6:9, 10:1, and 11:10. The second major section of the book is called the "Patriarchal History," with the same characteristic source title heading up the narratives about Abraham (11:27–25:11), Ishmael (25:12–18), Jacob (25:19–35:29), Esau (36:1–37:1) and Joseph (37:2–50:26). However, the cycles of Abraham, Jacob and Joseph are each given about ten or more chapters, so that they make up more than 60 percent of the book of Genesis. That is a fairly traditional way to view Genesis.

A better view of the book of Genesis is structured around four major periods: the Primeval Times, the Abrahamic Cycle, the Jacob Cycle and the Joseph Cycle, with four transitional sections,[2] between the four centers, ending in a Resolution Section. It could be outlined in this manner:

3

DESCRIPTION:	BIBLICAL REFERENCE:
1. The Primeval Times (Prologue)	Genesis 1:1–11:26
2. Transition (Genealogy)	Genesis 11:27–32
3. The Abrahamic Cycle	Genesis 12:1–25:11
4. Transition (Genealogy)	Genesis 25:12–18
5. The Jacob Cycle	Genesis 25:19–35:22b
6. Transition (Genealogy)	Genesis 35:22c–36:40
7. The Joseph Cycle	Genesis 37:1–46:7
8. Transition (Genealogy)	Genesis 46:8–27
9. The Resolution (Settlement in Egypt)	Genesis 46:28–50:26

In an attempt to determine how these four major periods gave us the beginnings and foundations for the material in Genesis, we need first of all to discuss the Hebrew word *toledoth*, which is translated "generations [of]" or "accounts [of]," as the indicator of the sources used for the four major cycles in Genesis.

Toledoth occurs thirty-nine times in the Bible, including twelve times in Numbers 1, where an enumeration of all the tribes appears, once in Numbers 3:1, nine times in 1 Chronicles, and Ruth 4:18ff lists the Davidic lineage from Perez down to David, Exodus 6:16 and 19 gives the "generations" of Levi and Exodus 28:10, which refers to Jacob's twelve sons. The rest of its occurrences appear thirteen times in Genesis (2:4; 5:1; 6:9; 10:1, 32; 11:10, 27; 25:12, 13, 19; 36:1, 9, 37:2). It seems this word indicated the sources that were used for the construction of the history of the cycles or periods of time.

To begin this discussion on the phrase "generations of," two scholars, P. J. Wiseman and R. K. Harrison, became the most active in their presentation of a case for the word *toledoth*. They both were insistent that eleven of the thirteen occurrences in Genesis marked the original tablets that functioned as the literary sources for writing the book.[3]

However, these two men also insisted that the references to the lines "These are the generations of" or "These are the accounts of" were colophons (section breaks) that came at the end of the texts they sourced in Genesis, rather than acting as headings or rubrics. But this does not seem to work out as these two scholars had imagined, for Genesis 25:12 has the *toledoth* of Ishmael, which if it is at the conclusion of that material in Genesis 11:27b–25:12, covers not the life or events of Ishmael, but instead describes the history of Abraham! Viewing these expressions as colophons, then, does not work at all; they are better viewed as rubrics or headings for the material that follows, not conclusions at the end of the material!

Moreover, such genealogical record-keeping as seen in Genesis is not unattested elsewhere in the Bible; it is replete with such genealogical records all through its pages. For example, such records were kept in Numbers, Ezra, Nehemiah, 1 Chronicles, Matthew and Luke. It may be that each family or clan kept in written form its own set of genealogical lists for their own family by updating it in each generation.

In this study, however, we shall be concerned mainly with the life and walk with God of the Patriarch Abraham, Genesis 12–25. The fact that he is called a "Patriarch" meant he was seen as a "father who rules." As such, he was the head of his family and household. It is true, of course, that these Patriarchs were migrant shepherds, whose main occupation was one of overseeing their flocks as they pastured on the grasslands available to them. But these men lived in the flourishing period archaeologists call the Middle Bronze Age (ca. 2166 to c. 1550 B.C.E.)—a time reputed to be one of especially high cultural achievement. In Egypt, for example, this also was the time of the Egyptian Middle Kingdom (Dynasty XII), which lasted from 1991 to 1786 B.C.E., an equally impressive period of art and literature.

This early biblical period yielded such archaeological evidence as the Code of Hammurabi, clay tablets from the Amorite city of Mari (Tell Hariri), as well as from Nuzi (the city of the biblical Horites), material from the city of Alalakh, and from the Syrian city of Ebla (Tell Mardikh). Nevertheless, despite such advances in culture of the general population, the patriarchal narratives depicted the lifestyle of these people as nomadic, for their care of sheep, goats and cattle meant they had to migrate over vast areas of land, usually staying at each place for a rather short period of time.

The best evidence for such geographical migration and the levels of cultural attainment can best be seen on the wall mural in a tomb at Beni Hasan, dating from about 1892 B.C.E It depicts a parade of thirty-seven Asiatics from the region of Shut (the areas of southern Canaan and Sinai) led by their chief Abishai, who was on his way to trade in Egypt. All thirty-seven Asiatics are dressed in colorful bright-striped clothes. The men wore knee-length skirts and sandals with shoes that covered the entire foot. Some were portrayed as blacksmiths, others were depicted as musicians playing various instruments, and others were portrayed as merchants with goods, presumably for sale, loaded on the backs of donkeys. This mural seems to match the description given in Genesis 4:21–22.

Abram was known and previously called in Deuteronomy 26:5 "a wandering Aramean" (cf. Psalm 105:12), i.e., one who wandered from nation to nation. But he was also known as a "prophet" (Genesis 20:7), which means "one called by God." That call was repeated and reaffirmed to Abram in Genesis 12:1–3, 7; 15:5–21; 17:4–8; 18:18–19; 22:17–18 as well as repeated later on of his son Isaac in Genesis 26:2–4 and then on to Jacob in Genesis 28:13–15; 35:11–12; and 46:3. The call to Abram involved seven promises: (1) the land, (2) descendants, (3) blessedness, (4) fame, (5) opportunity for service, (6) protection, and (7) universal influence.

Let us begin our study of this man Abraham and the part he played in the Patriarchal Era.

Lesson 1

The Call of Abram

Genesis 11:27–12:9

Chronological Details of Abraham's Family

The scope of the Abrahamic narrative is clearly delineated in an inclusion by two source formulas. The first rubric was "This is the account of Terah's family." Terah became the father of Abram, Nahor, and Haran" as recorded in 11:27. The second rubric was "This is the account of the family line of Abraham's son Ishmael, whom Sarah's servant, Hagar the Egyptian, bore to Abraham," as 25:12 parenthetically notes. Abram's story preceded the Jacob narrative (Genesis 25–35) and the Joseph account (Genesis 37–50), in which both followed the Abrahamic cycle. What was common to all three cycles, however, was the "father" was the head of the family and the principal hero; this is why we call these "patriarchal narratives."

The transitional material of Genesis 11:27–32 informs us that Terah had three sons, Abraham, Nahor and Haran. Haran went on to bear his son, Lot (27b), but Haran later died in the land of the Chaldeans. Meanwhile, Abram married Sarai, and Nahor married Milkah. Terah then took his son Abram, his daughter-in-law Sarai and his grandson Lot, and they left Ur, a city of the Chaldeans, intending to go to Canaan. However, they stopped at Haran, where they settled down, and where Terah died after living for 205 years without ever having reached the Promised Land of Canaan, even though they left Ur with the firm decision to go there!

Divine Promises to Abraham – 12:1–3, 7

In the New Testament, Stephen, whom the apostles had appointed a deacon, defending his actions and beliefs before the Sanhedrin, declared:

> The God of glory appeared to our father Abraham while he was still in Mesopotamia, before he lived in Haran. "Leave your country and your people," God said, "and go to the land I will show you." (Acts 7:2b–3)

Again, it is puzzling why Terah never finished his journey to Canaan, for we are never given a reason; it merely says he "settled there" in Haran

(11:31). But it was Abram who was the one who seemed to be the one who ended up being specially called by God to go to Canaan, for in Genesis 12:1 he was divinely ordered:

> Get thee out of thy country, and from thy kindred, and from thy father's house [in Haran?], unto the land that I will show thee . . ." (KJV)

The prophet Isaiah likewise affirmed Abram's divine call in these words:

> Listen to me, you who pursue righteousness
>   and seek the LORD.
> Look to the rock from which you were cut
>   and to the quarry from which you were hewn;
> Look to Abraham, your father,
>   and to Sarah, who gave birth.
> When I called him he was only one man,
>   and I blessed him and made him many. (Isaiah 51:1–2, NIV)

The same Lord, who would later also call men like the prophet Elijah from Tishbe of Gilead, the prophet Elisha from his father's farm in Abel Meholah, the prophet Amos from Tekoa, the Apostle Peter from his fishing nets, Matthew from his toll collecting booth, or even Cromwell from his farm in Huntingdon, or Martin Luther from his cloister in Erfurt—this same God had also earlier called Abraham.[1]

Most regard Genesis 12:1–3, then, as expressing the quintessence of the theology that lies at the heart of the Abrahamic story. What Abraham is promised here is exactly what one monarch after another hoped his rule would produce, these four gifts from God: nationhood, a great name, divine protection, and the means of being the conduit for blessing others! Each of these gifts from the Lord may now be examined.

Abram would spend most of his time in Hebron, in the southern part of Canaan. Abram was also called "the friend of God," a name applied to him in 2 Chronicles 20:7. There King Jehoshaphat prayed:

> Our God, did you not drive out the inhabitants of this land, before the people of Israel and give it forever to the descendants of Abraham your friend.

Again, that same title is given to Abraham in Isaiah 41:8.

> But you, Israel, my servant, Jacob, whom I have chosen, you descendants of Abraham my friend.

This same title is also used in the New Testament for Abraham in James 2:23.

> And the Scripture was fulfilled that says, "Abraham believed God, and it was credited to him as righteousness," and he was called "God's friend."

No wonder, then, that the town of Hebron was also known by the Arabic name El Khalil, meaning "the Friend"—an obvious reference to Abraham.

A Great Nation

This same promise was repeated to Abraham in Genesis 18:18; then to Ishmael in Genesis 17:20 and 21:18, later to Jacob in Genesis 46:3, and then to Moses in Exodus 32:10. This would mean that those to whom this word was promised could look forward to a large population, an extensive territory, and spiritual development. Greatness would come from God himself!

A Great Name

Usually in Scripture, only the name of God is great (Joshua 7:9; 1 Samuel 12:22; Malachi 1:11), but such a hope for greatness was the dream of many a royal person in antiquity and some in the modern era as well. However, in Scripture the promise of "making one's name great" seemed to be restricted to the themes found in the Abrahamic and Davidic covenants (2 Samuel 7:9); therefore, the purpose was not to merely exalt the man *per se*, but to show God's endorsement of the one called and his actions as part of the Promise-Plan of God. Their "name" stood for their reputation and honor as part of God's Promise-Plan.

I Will Curse Whoever Disdains You

God promised to provide his protection by actively intervening for his people Israel. Those who opposed Abram were said to "disdain" him. In Genesis 12:3, God used the strong term *'arar*, "to curse." This speaks of a judgment that God will render on the wicked. (God is saying, "I will bitterly curse whoever disdains you.")

Bless You

It is clear that the Hebrew root word that means "to bless" is the prominent feature of this divine covenant with Abraham, for it occurs five times in vv. 2–3—perhaps to offset the five curses mentioned in the previous section of Genesis. Moreover, this Hebrew root, "to bless," appears more times in Genesis than in any other part of Scripture—some 88 times out of the 310 throughout the rest of the Old Testament. God's blessing can be seen in such things as one's health, long life, peace, prosperity, good harvests and children. But carefully note: God alone is the source of such good gifts, not "luck," one's own "drive," "success," or hard work!

The Niphal form of this verb, "to bless," appears only three times in the Old Testament (Genesis 12:3; 18:18; 28:14). The Septuagint, Vulgate and the Jewish *Targum Onkelos* correctly render it as a passive verb, "be blessed"—by God, of course. But others see it as a reflexive verb, saying in effect, "May we bless ourselves just as Abram did," as if mortals would use Abram's name in blessing themselves and each other, or Abram was able to bless himself.

Abram's Response to God's Call

God commanded Abram to "Go," or perhaps even more dramatically, "Get out," of your father's household (12:1). "So, Abram went, as the LORD had told him" (12:4). Abraham is seen as one who was most obedient to the divine commands (Genesis 17:23). Some feel that Abram left Haran sixty years before his father died, but Acts 7:4 seems to indicate that Abram only left Haran *after* his father died. Thus, Genesis 11:27 must mean that Terah began "having children" (Hebrew *yalad*) when he was 70 years old, without giving a precise time when each of the three sons were born, which in Abram's case would have meant that he was actually born when Terah was 130 years old, and not in his 70th year.

Verse 5 makes it clear that Terah set out to go to Canaan; however, he settled down in Haran, and there he ended his days. While in Haran, Abram acquired "property" (Hebrew *rekush*, i.e., "moveable property"), which included herds as well as "servants" (Hebrew *nepheshim*). For the second time, it also mentions the fact that Lot went with Abram, for there must have been a close relationship between Abram and his nephew Lot.

"Abram traveled through the land [of Canaan]" in v. 6, thereby indicating he must have journeyed south from Haran through the city of Damascus, passing by the north side of the Sea of Galilee as he moved west on to the city of Shechem, which is just east of modern-day Nablus. Joshua claimed that Shechem lay in the middle of the land of Canaan (Joshua 20:7). At that city there was the "oak of Moreh," perhaps the same tree as mentioned in Judges 9:37. *Moreh* literally means "teacher," which may indicate, according to some, that this was a place where one went to obtain a divine oracle. But more likely is the fact it was the place where the Lord would appear. Of course, all this took place while the Canaanites were living in the land.

The Promise of the Land of Canaan

Verse 7 has the first recorded instance of the Lord appearing to a patriarch (Genesis 17:1; 18:1; 26:2, 24; 35:9; 48:3), but later on the Lord will appear at Sinai and then in the Tabernacle. Here in v. 7 we have the first of what will be close to 200 repetitions of the promise of the land of Canaan to Abram throughout Genesis (Genesis 13:14–15, 17:15:7, 13, 16, 18; 17:8; 26:2–3), which had already been implied in Genesis 12:1–2. Some, such as Westermann,[2] argue that this promise of the land was secondary, despite the vast number of times this promise was repeated! But that hardly matches the plethora of instances this promise appears all the way through the prophets!

The Building of an Altar

"So [Abram] built an altar there to the LORD, who had appeared to him" (12:7c). Therefore, Abram's first act was to build an altar after he had reached his goal in the land. We may assume that he also offered a sacrifice on it, just as Noah had done as soon as he came out of the ark (Genesis 8:20). If we want to trace the journeys of Abram through the land, we should "follow the altars," for he went on to build altars at Bethel, Hebron, and on Mount Moriah (12:8; 13:18; 22:9). The other patriarchs followed suit, as Isaac built one at Beersheba (26:25), Jacob at Luz (35:7), and even Moses built one at Rephidim (Exodus 17:15, 24:4). Abram's construction of the altar signified that he believed God when he promised to give him the land of Canaan, even though Abram did not take possession of it at that time.

Abram moved on from Shechem, which is situated in a valley between Mount Gerizim and Mount Ebal, then he went on to "the hills east of Bethel" (12:8). Formerly Bethel was called Luz (28:19), but its newer name was used here as an anticipation of the later change of name. Bethel is usually identified with Beitin, some 10 miles north of Jerusalem. But the site of Ai is more difficult, for while it once was identified by scholars with the site of Et-Tell, about one and a half miles from Beitin, it has no remains from the start of the Early Bronze Age until the Iron Age, which precluded this site from being the place of Ai when it was vacant during the time of the events identified with it. However, recently Bethel's location has been reset at El-Bireh, two miles south of Beitin, and Ai is now relocated to Khirbet Nisya, a mile southeast of El-Bireh.[3]

Conclusion

Genesis 12:1–9 prominently displays God's divine call and Abraham's response. These opening words on the life of Abraham describe the Lord's command to leave Abram's home originally located in Ur of the Chaldees, but later in Haran, and then to undertake the long journey in obedient faith.

The list of promises mentioned in this section of Genesis meant that they would be given to Abraham from the hand of God. Abraham acknowledged this by his acts of worship as he traversed the land of Canaan almost from one end to the other, thereby showing he knew the extent of the promise God had made to him. As part of these promises, this man was to father children, inherit a land especially reserved for him and his descendants, enjoy divine protection, and be the source of blessing to the whole world. As such, he would be the first of the Pilgrim Fathers who would blaze the trail for others who would follow.

Questions for Thought or Discussion

1. Can you suggest a reason why Terah stopped in Haran for the rest of his life and never went on to Canaan as God had called him?
2. How important a factor is the blessing of God for the world in the rest of Scripture?
3. Can you guess why Lot was so closely associated with Abram and not his own father Haran?
4. Why is the land promise so important in this text, in the rest of Scripture and in history?

Lesson 2

Abram Goes to Egypt

Genesis 12:10–20

Now there was a famine in the land, and Abram went down to Egypt to live there for a while because the famine was severe. – Genesis 12:10

"Now there was a famine in the land" (12:10). A famine in the land of Promise? That is surprising! Had Abram made a mistake in going to Canaan? Had God been aware that he was going to allow a famine to occur in the land to which he was sending Abram and his family? If he did know this—and how could a sovereign God not—what was his purpose in allowing this to happen? What was he trying to show Abram? Or was Abram out of the will of God in going to Egypt?

Perhaps to justify Abram's descent into Egypt, we are told: "He went down to Egypt to live there for a while because the famine was severe" (12:10b). One can only imagine how such a trip into a strange land was filled with adventure and mystery, for already Egypt would have existed from years prior to that as seen in the pyramids, the Sphinx, and of course the bountiful Nile River that annually flooded the long narrow strip of land on each side of its banks, making it a fruitful area of vegetation. No wonder, then, that Egypt was regarded as one of the granaries of the world.

But there was no clear word that Abram received an explicit divine directive to go down to Egypt during this time. He may have acted on his own judgment as he saw the emerging difficulty of the famine and its approaching severity. He may have become overcome with fear for the lives of his family and himself, because of the intensity of the famine. After all, he had just arrived in the Land of Promise, armed with the promises and the call of God, but there is no evidence of any such instruction to leave Canaan and go to Egypt!

There are, however, just such occasions in the biblical narrative where God himself on other occasions did directly order his servants to seek temporary refuge and asylum in Egypt. For example, did not God own the waters of the Nile River; therefore, they were just as much a provision from his hand as were the seasonal and more frequent rains in Canaan.

We can also recall later examples of such explicit directions from God to send his servant(s) into Egypt. For example, what about the time the Lord directed the Patriarch Jacob to join his recently discovered son Joseph, now in charge of distributing the grain in Egypt? Did not the Lord say to Jacob, "I am God, the God of your father. . . . Do not be afraid to go down to Egypt, for I will make you into a great nation there. I will go down to Egypt with you, and I will surely bring you back again [to Canaan]" (Genesis 46:3–4)?

So, Jacob went to Egypt under the explicit instructions from God. Later, in New Testament times, did not the Lord appear to Joseph and Mary, after the wise men had left Herod's palace to visit the house where Mary, Joseph and the baby Yeshua were staying, and say, through the angel of the Lord, "Get [out of here] . . .Take the child and his mother and escape to Egypt. Stay there until I tell you, for Herod is going to search for the child to kill him" (Matthew 2:13).

Accordingly, we may assume that there may be times in our lives, just as it was in the lives of those already cited, that God may clearly indicate that it is his will for us to go away from Canaan into the world at large, using Egypt as a metaphor for this world and its culture, for the Lord has some definite plan in mind and a purpose he wishes us to accomplish. In this way, Israel and all believers of all ages are invited to see in Abram's experience in Egypt an adumbration of not only the future exodus of Israel from Egypt under God's mighty hand, but of Yeshua's exodus from Egypt, as well (Matthew 2:15), or the similar experience of the Church's experience in Messiah (1 Corinthians 10:1–12).

In fact, John Sailhamer argues that this account of Abram in Egypt has the marks on it of having been "intentionally shaped to parallel the later account of God's majestic and renowned deliverance of Israel from Egypt (Genesis 41–Exodus 12)."[1] He illustrates this with a chart matching the phrases from Genesis 12:10–20 in parallelism with those in Genesis 41:54b to 47:27 and Exodus 11:1–12:47. Sailhamer comments:

> The whole of God's plan, from beginning to end, is contained within the scope of this simple story. In light of these parallels we should also understand the close similarity between the account of Abram's sojourn in Egypt in chapter 12, the account of his sojourn in Gerar in chapter 20, and the account of Isaac's sojourn in Gerar in chapter 26. . . . We cannot

be content merely to reduce the importance of the similarities to evidence for a "common tradition," nor is it enough to attribute the similarities to mere coincidence. It is likely that the similarities are intentional and part of a larger pattern of "parallel narratives" distributed compositionally throughout the Pentateuch.[2]

Sailhamer goes on to point out how the Joseph narratives in Genesis exhibit such noticeable "sets" of parallel dreams, each with a number of similarities. Even though the dreams differ in some of their details, each "set" of dreams was related to the same set of circumstances.

The Threat of a Famine

This would not be the last time that the people of promise were faced with the warning of a famine, or of other such types of judgments, for such terminology also appears in Genesis 26:1; 41:54, 56; 43:1, not to mention the rest of Scripture. So severe were those times of threatening famine that they often compelled the patriarchs and their families to leave Canaan (47:4; cf. Ruth 1:1), usually fleeing to Egypt.

The problem of each of these threats was that they had the possibility of endangering the Promises of God; indeed, this would be a recurrent theme in the narratives that appeared throughout Genesis. Thus, the present story was not an exception to this threat, for if Abram and his family liked the good life in Egypt and refused to leave Egypt, then what would become of God's Promise-Plan for them and later generations? Abram illustrates this well, for he also later on faced the threat of Sarai's barrenness, his loss of his good name, the loss of his land and the loss of his herds. In the face of such threats, God nevertheless played a central role by directly entering the scene to fulfill and maintain his divine promise as examples of his grace and mercy.

A Dependence on God Rather Than on Himself

But what if Abram committed an awful mistake by going down to Egypt when God had not commanded him to do so? Our Lord was able to use Abram's error as a later teaching incident for future parallel incidents, yet Abram, in a moment of panic, may have adopted his own method of delivering himself from the threat of a severe famine, instead of throwing the responsibility back on the God who had called him. Would that not be similar to later events in the modern era, where believing young ladies often plunged into marriage with unsaved mates only to court future disaster, because their motivation was to get married so as to avoid being tagged as an "old maid"? Ah, what a disastrous mistake if that was the reason for their action. Of course, what was common to both Abram, had he gone ahead on his own instincts to solve his problem, as we often do, was the desire to trust his own guidance and not the guidance that comes from our Lord. In a similar vein, believing merchants occasionally take on an ungodly partner for the sake of raising capital that these new partners might bring into the relationship. Believers must be careful not to court the help of the world if they are not explicitly directed to do so by the God who called them into that work.

Would it not have been better for Abram to have thrown the responsibility back on the Lord, and to say to him something like this: "Lord, you have brought me to this land of Canaan; now I need you to instruct me in this crisis of a coming severe famine. I will remain here until I know exactly what I and my family are to do now." Certainly our Lord can be trusted in the difficulties of life just as he is dependable for the ordinary affairs of each day.

One Failure Often Leads to Another

If our supposition about Abram failing to seek God's will on whether he should have gone down to Egypt or not is correct (and we certainly cannot prove that it was!), then what happened to him next follows and makes more sense. That is to say, when he lost his trust in seeking direction from the Lord, he also seems to have lost his courage concerning God's ability to preserve him and his wife in the strange settings of the land of Egypt.

No doubt Abram had heard of the licentiousness of the Egyptians and feared for his own life at the hands of potentially mendacious predators who would see the obvious beauty of his wife, leading them to take her as one of their wives! What Abram feared, however, actually happened, for "the Egyptians saw that [Sarai] was a very beautiful woman" (12:14). Even Pharaoh's officials had the same opinion and thoughts about her, for they bragged about her to Pharaoh, who then took her into his palace. To be sure, Abram was treated well for her sake (12:14), but that is because he had told Pharaoh's officials that Sarai was his "sister" (12:13), a game of deception she followed at Abram's command. In the meantime, Abram acquired "sheep and cattle, male and female donkeys, menservants and maidservants, and camels" (12:16) as presents for his "sister."

Of course, there was an element of truth in Abram's claim, for Sarai was his half-sister. But Pharaoh eventually saw that it was meant to deceive and mislead him. Moreover, it put at risk the promised seed that God had already spoken about to Abram—if not his whole Promise-Plan. As it so often happens, we mortals are all too willing to sacrifice all that is nearest and dearest to us in the Gospel of our Lord in exchange for other temporary gifts. Abram had been treated royally by Pharaoh's gifts (12:16), but they were poor substitutes for inexpressibly greater gifts and being chosen by our Lord to be the means of blessing the whole world.

The Scriptures do not hesitate or shrink back from relating the sins of even its noblest characters such as Abram. This is another indication of the Bible's veracity and truthfulness—it says it like it is! This should be an encouragement to us. Moreover, if God can take such human material, as obviously Abram was made of, and call him his "friend" (Isaiah 41:8), and still make out of him his servant and use him to carry out his Promise-Plan, then is he not able to do the same for us even though we may have also grievously sinned against him? Still, the one key response God expects of all of us is full surrender to his will and obedience by faith to his Word.

Did the Patriarchs Have Domesticated Camels?

This narrative of the patriarchs takes for granted that Abram and the patriarchs had "camels" (Hebrew *gemalim*) that were domesticated for the patriarchs' use. "Camels" appears in the Pentateuch twenty-eight times for a total of some fifty-seven times in the Old Testament. This means that forty-nine percent of the references (28 of 57) relate to the Patriarchal age. They appear most prominently in the Patriarchal account of Abram (12:6), Isaac (24:10) and Jacob (31:34). However, twentieth-century scholars began to teach that the archaeological and epigraphic materials from this period of the Middle or Late Bronze Periods did not support the domestication of the camel before 1200 B.C.E.

Nevertheless, such claims of anachronisms in the patriarchal record have been challenged by conservative scholars, who point to the domestication of camels, even if it is only on a limited scale in the Middle Bronze and Late Bronze Ages. Moreover, research has shown that we must distinguish between two types of camels in the Ancient Near East, the dromedary (i.e., the long-legged single-hump camel) and the Bactrian camel (the stocky type with two humps). Some argue for the fact that the Bactrian camel was domesticated before the later training of the dromedary, but that fact is now challenged with evidence from lower Mesopotamia and southern Arabia that such domestication of both types may easily go back to 2500 B.C.E. Randall Younker has also shown from some petroglyphs depicting camels being led by humans in Wadi Nasib, Sinai, which he dates no later than 1500 B.C.E.[3]

The evidence for the camel's bones in the Middle Bronze layers is now verified for archaeological layers at Gezer, Megiddo, Taanach, and in Late Bronze at Tell Jemmeh. The camel's domestication is known from the Old Babylonian period from a Sumerian lexical text from Ugarit. Another Sumerian text from Nippur and from the same period of time references awareness of camels' milk. However, the use of the camel both for domestic and military activities during the later Iron Age is now well-known. Thus, we may conclude that the camel was well-known in the earlier periods prior to the third millennium B.C.E. in most parts of the ancient Near East.

Finally, we note that though the Hebrews were permitted to use the camel for transportation, they were not permitted to eat its meat. The camel was labeled as "unclean" because, although it chews its cud, it does not have a split hoof (Leviticus 11:4; Deuteronomy 14:7). Nor can it be taken for granted that camels' milk could be drunk by Israelites, even though there is a reference to Jacob's thirty "milk camels with their colts" (Genesis 32:14). But this text has reference to "nursing" female camels. 2 Kings 1:8 and Zechariah 13:4 do show that some Israelites may have worn rough camel skins, but that seems to be the extent of it.

Conclusions

1. It still appears that Abram should have consulted God first before he went down into Egypt; why else would the narrator attach, alongside the text about the famine, the story about Abram exposing his wife to harm when Pharaoh almost made Sarai his wife?

2. The fact that God sent a severe famine just as Abram was entering the land of Canaan is cause for pause. Was God already testing just how much his man Abram trusted him?

3. What would have happened to God's Promise-Plan had Pharaoh married Sarai and taken her away from Abram? How would the Gospel have been impacted?

4. Why does this text note that Lot went with Abram to Egypt (13:1)?

Questions for Thought or Discussion

1. What is your estimate as to whether Abram and Sarai went to Egypt with the permission of God or as evidence of a lack of faith?
2. If God did not direct Abram to go to Egypt, why did he still go there when he knew the risk he was posing for his wife Sarai and the Promise-Plan of God?
3. Why is the domestication of camels such an important item in the patriarchal story?
4. How did the large number of gifts that Pharaoh gave to Abram figure into the wealth that came from God?
5. Why did God "inflict serious diseases" on the Egyptians since Abram had gone to Egypt in disobedience to God?
6. Did Abram and Sarai do the right thing by going to Egypt, or did they sin and show a spirit of worldliness, as some charge?
7. How did Abram's lie to Pharaoh almost cost the fulfillment of all that God had promised him in his covenant?
8. Is Abram a type of Messiah in any way in this passage?

Lesson 3

Abram and Lot Separate

Genesis 13:1–18

So, Abram said to Lot, "Let's not have any quarreling between you and me, or between your herders and mine, for we are closer relatives."
– Genesis 13:9

Heretofore, Abram and Lot had worked together quite amicably, but apparently the time had come for Uncle Abram and his nephew Lot to separate. What may seem to only be an aside story from the private life of Abram in Genesis 13, actually is a place in Scripture where we readers are taught opportunities—to practice generosity, justice, mercy, and moderation—along with learning how piety and affection can go together, as well as forbearance and forgiveness.

Pharaoh, after learning he had been fooled by Abram, had his men "send [Abram] away [along with] his wife and all that he had" (12:20). The Lord had indeed "plagued Pharaoh and his house with great plagues because of Sarai, Abram's wife" (12:17). Pharaoh must have been mad as hops to have been taken in and tricked by Abram and Sarai. I sense that he may have spoken roughly to Abram as he ordered him to take his wife and get out of Egypt as fast as they could (12:19).

Back to Where Abram's Tent Was at the Beginning

I imagine, therefore, that Abram left Egypt as speedily as he could, but with all the gifts in hand that Pharaoh had given him. Pharaoh's mind may have been so occupied with the thought of halting the plague that he had to do anything he could to stop the outbreak of disease in Egypt. He wanted that whole retinue to leave as fast as they could. So Abram left Egypt along with his brother's son Lot and all his newly acquired possessions.

So, he left Egypt and went back, first into the southern part of Canaan. Since no mention had been made of Lot being in Egypt, even though he had been with Abram during that time, it was necessary for the narrator to bring him back into the narrative once again by reintroducing him (13:1b).

Abram continued through the southern part of Canaan in a northern direction until he came to the place, between Bethel and Ai, "where his tent had been at the beginning," before he went down into Egypt (v. 3). Once Abram and his retinue had arrived in Bethel, he came to the place of the altar.

The fact that he returned to the spot where he had set up an altar may well indicate that the altar and the worship of his Lord were the main attractions that drew him to that spot between Bethel and Ai. If so, this would indicate that Abram's heart was set not on his earthly assets but upon his spiritual inheritance, the place where he perhaps remembered the delight he had had as he worshiped at the altar and enjoyed fellowship with the Lord. This site near Bethel, then, may have endeared itself to the patriarch as one filled with vivid memories of meeting his Lord there. Thus, Abram may have been able to sing along with the sons of Korah in Psalm 84:1–2,

> How lovely is your dwelling place, LORD Almighty!
> My soul yearns, even faints,
> for the courts of the LORD;
> My heart and my flesh cry out
> for the Living God.

It was at Bethel that Abram called on the name of the Lord (v. 4b). This calling on the Lord's name took priority in Abram's life, for his private and public worship of God would continue to take a top seat in his list of activities.

Meanwhile, we are told in verse 5 that Lot, who continued to accompany Abram, also had flocks, herds and tents. The word "tents" stood for the occupants of those tents, i.e., his wife Sarai, children and domestics, as was used in 1 Chronicles 4:41 as well.

Wealthy Abram

We are not told how many cattle or flocks this patriarch had, but if the story of Job 1:3 is any measure for that period of time, it must have been considerable. Genesis 13:2 says, "Abram was very rich in cattle, in silver, and in gold." Whether it could be rightly judged that he went down into Egypt a man poor in cattle and with very little gold or silver, we cannot say. However, Lot must have inherited from his father considerable wealth, for his herds were competing with Abram's for pasture and water.

The interesting fact is that God had promised Abram that he would "bless him" (Genesis 12:2). Is it possible that this was one of the ways that

God increased Abram's holdings by having Pharaoh give him a load of gifts, even though they were given as a result of this patriarch's deceit? Since the Egyptians hated pastoral pursuits, it may be that they did not see these gifts as valuable as they actually were, but as God permitted him to possess them, they became part of his blessing from God rather than from Pharaoh.

The Separation of Abram and Lot

The fact that the land was unable to support both of them speaks volumes to the size of their herds (v. 6a), for "their possessions (or "acquisitions") were so great that they were not able to stay together" (v. 6b). Given the increasing scarcity of pasturage, along with the limited amount of water for the cattle, strife broke out between Abram's and Lot's herdsmen. As a result of this pressure, now resting on both groups of herdsmen, opposition, anger, wrath and petulance became the order of the day between the two factions. The mischief arising from such bitter challenges exchanged between the two sides could not be contained within the limits of just these two households. However, even something this small could only have future consequences that would be trouble for both sides, for verse 7b notes almost as an aside, "The Canaanites and Perizzites were also living in the land at that time." Should these foreigners decide to take advantage of the distraction these adversaries were showing against each other, it would result in more trouble than either of them wanted.

Mercifully, Abram stepped in to ease the inflamed hostilities by saying, "Let's not have any quarreling between you [Lot] and me, or between your herdsmen and mine, for we are close relatives. Is not the whole land before you? Let's part company. If you go to the left, I'll go to the right; if you go to the right, I'll go to the left" (vv. 8–9). Abram was certainly a "relative," for he was an uncle to Lot and also a brother-in-law to him, for he also had married Lot's sister. But even beyond this family relationship, they were "brethren" in an even higher sense, for they both professed the same faith and the same kind of worship at the altar. Thus, as advocates of faith and worship in the same Lord, they owed to each other love, peace and good will. As F. B. Meyer opines:

> Entangled in an alliance which you seem powerless to break off, your only hope is to bear it quietly 'til God sets you at liberty. Meanwhile, guard your will, by God's grace, from swinging round, as a boat with the

tide. . . . Wait patiently 'til God's hour strikes, and his hand opens the fast-locked door, and bids you enter free. That time will come at length; for God has a destiny in store for you, so great that neither He nor you can allow it to be forfeited for any light or trivial obstacle.[1]

Here is one of the great teachings of our faith: As members of the same spiritual family, we are bound to become in all things brethren to each other. Moreover, we are bound not only by the bonds of believers' fraternity, but even more so by the bonds of being part of the body of Messiah. Where then would there be room for divisions of heart, bitterness of feelings, and strife between our brotherhood? How can we permit the bonds of tranquility to be ruptured and alienated no matter how serious the fault, when our Lord has paid so much to bring us together as brethren?

The Practical Nature of Abram's Kindness

Many commentators rightly point out that there is no finer example of a generous spirit in a mortal than that which Abram exhibits in verses 9–10. In fact, it was right at this point of one of the most trying situations where Abram could have demanded what had been given already as a gift from God. But instead of demanding that he, as the elder of the two and as the recipient of the gift of the land—indeed, the one distinctly called by God—be favored, Abram deferred and submitted to his nephew's wishes by giving him the right of first choice. Instead of Abram arrogating the right to himself, he evidenced a spirit of gentleness that taught that being a servant to all is the spirit that most closely approximates the character of our Lord. This avoided further angry disputes and bitter hostilities by placing in the forefront a proposal of peace.

Surely Lot could not help but know there was an enormous difference in the quality of the lands he would choose. Lot ended up "look[ing] around" and "see[ing] that the whole plain of Jordan," for it was "well-watered like the garden of the LORD" (v. 10). Lot's actions here are in striking contrast with Abram's, for Lot exhibited selfishness and concerns for his own interests as he greedily snatched up the best and most fertile areas. Lot surely was culpable, for he did not give priority to the need of his soul, but only that which his eyes could see and what he could achieve with such luscious green fertile pasturage.

The River Jordan and the alluvial plain it had produced were the obvious prizes if one were to choose that real estate over the mountainous regions of the rest of Canaan. But that feature of natural lushness alone was not as significant to Abram as was his walk with God!

Conclusions

1. The difference between Abram's choice and Lot's choice revealed what was in the character of each man.
2. Abram's choice did not indicate that he was a failure or that he failed to believe God's promises when he gave Lot the first choice and was left with the land of Canaan, which was not as productive and fertile!

Questions for Thought or Discussion

1. Where did Abram go after he left Egypt, and why did he make that choice? Does his choice say anything about his attitude toward God?
2. Judging from Abram and Lot's choice of portions of the land, do they reveal anything about their attitudes towards wealth?
3. What criteria did Lot use in making his choice of the portion he would take of the land?
4. How did Abram go about determining God's will for his life? What helps does that offer to us in making similar decisions about the will of God?

Lesson 4

Abram Rescues Lot and Is Blessed by Melchizedek

Genesis 14:1–24

> When Abram heard that his relative had been taken captive, he called out the 318 trained men born in his household and [he] went in pursuit [of them] as far as Dan. During the night Abram divided his men to attack them and he routed them as far as Hobah, north of Damascus. He recovered all the goods and brought back his relative Lot and his possessions, together with the women and the other people. – Genesis 14:14–16

It has been a part of critical scholarship to question the historicity and antiquity of the patriarchal narratives, particularly as argued by the Copenhagen minimalist school in archaeology and history. Nevertheless, this fourteenth chapter of Genesis has been a good example to use for making the case for the historical sources showing the reality of this story.

The first seventeen verses of Genesis 14 record how, in lower Canaan, on the shores of the southeastern part of the Dead Sea, the five cities of the Jordanian plain were invaded by a coalition of four Mesopotamian kings. Lot, Abram's nephew, had been living in Sodom, one of the five cities, but he and his entire household were captured and taken as hostages by these four kings (v. 12). But Abram and his 318 "armed retainers" caught up with the hostile coalition by springing a surprise night attack on the kings and their armies, who were sleeping near the northern town of Dan. Abram soundly defeated them and retook all they had taken in their conquest from the five cities of the plain where Lot had chosen to pasture his flocks.

The scriptural account of this battle gives a precise list of names and places, often including both their foreign or original names along with their more local or contemporary names. For example, "the Vale of Siddim" is also given more-contemporary names such as "the Dead Sea Valley" (v. 3), and "the Valley of Shaveh" is also called "the King's Valley" (v. 17). Such traits identify this passage as reflecting earlier antiquity. Even though the names of the four kings have not yet been identified in any cuneiform documents, their names are typical of that time and place.

The Four Mesopotamian Kings – 14:1–4 [1]

It is not clear whether "Amraphel king of Shinar," who is mentioned in this chapter first, or Chedorlaomer king of Elam, was the head of this coalition of four kings. But what is clear is that five kings—Bera of Sodom, Birsha of Gomorrah, Shinab of Adamah, Shemeber of Zeboiim, and the king of Bela, also known as the city or town of Zoar—had all revolted against these Mesopotamian oppressors. After paying tribute for twelve years to Chedorlaomer (which may indicate that he indeed was chief in this coalition), in the thirteenth year they refused to do so any longer (v. 4). In the ancient Near East, such a refusal to pay a tribute was usually a sign of a rebellion, as was the case when Hezekiah refused to give tribute to the Assyrian king (2 Kings 18:7).

The War of the Four Kings Versus the Five Cities of Jordan – 14:5–16

The fight recorded in Genesis 14 was more than just a skirmish about the border. It was an expedition led, it seems, by Chedorlaomer, the Napoleon of his times. Chedorlaomer's capital city was Susa, which laid across the desert and the Tigris River in Elam. Even before Abram had entered Canaan, this conqueror had already swept south previously, subduing towns in the Jordan Valley. Thus, when Lot took up his residence in Sodom, these cities of the plain were already paying tribute to this monarch and his allies.

But the men and women of Sodom, Gomorrah, Admah, and Zebooim had had enough, so they revolted after twelve years of heavy taxation. Chedorlaomer undertook a second expedition to punish these cities for their revolt and to regain his power and authority. So he, with three other vassal and friendly powers from the Euphrates Valley, whom he picked up as he moved in a westerly direction from Elam (also known as Persia), ravaged the country alongside these Jordanian towns that were the targets of his attack. Chedorlaomer smote the Rephaim, the Zuzim, and the Emim (v. 5).

Later, when Israel was about to cross over the Jordan River to own the land of Canaan, the half-tribe of Manasseh was given the city of Ashteroth. The Zuzim and Emim were both dispossessed of their territory by the children of Moab and Ammon, the later sons of Lot.

Accordingly, these invading Mesopotamian chiefs appear to have taken over the eastern bank of the Jordan from its source at the Sea of Galilee to the desert south of Canaan. After satisfying their quest for war in these areas, they apparently turned north to the Valley of the Jordan to take on the four kings of the plain. The Emim were said to dwell in Shaveh Kiriathaim, i.e., the plains or flats of Kiriathaim (v. 5b). These invaders had gone as far south as Mount Seir, where the Horites lived. The name "Horites" implies they were cave-dwellers (v. 6), but now the invaders would turn about and head north into the Valley of Jordan. The name "En-mishpat," literally "fountain of judgment," seems to anticipate the name that was conferred upon that place after Moses and Aaron sinned against God, striking the rock to produce water (Numbers 20:10). Because of his disobedience, Moses was prohibited from entering the Promised Land.

But now the battle was joined in the Valley of Siddim, a place of pits of oil and bitumen. This seemed to indicate that asphalt or bitumen just oozed up out of the ground, thereby being as much a problem for the invaders as it was for the inhabitants, who were trying to flee. The houses in Sodom might have been covered with such flammable matter, which made them all the more vulnerable when the fire began to overspread the city (v. 10).

No doubt Chedorlaomer encountered difficulty with the five cities' soil, because of the many bitumen pits. Moreover, it seems that the men who lived in the plain were too weak to resist; their moral corruption was but a harbinger of the political overthrow they would experience. The five cities were soundly defeated, their people captured, and their goods carried off (v. 11), while others were slain, and their bodies left in the abandoned towns.

The foreign troops began their slow homeward march back to Mesopotamia. Lot, Abram's brother, Nahor's son, who had taken up a residence in Sodom, was among the captives (v. 12). As Proverbs 13:20 later observes, the companion of fools will be destroyed, and that is what happened. Lot, the man who had proudly picked out the best grassland and country for his flocks and herds in the plains of Jordan, had not judged what impact such a move would have on his spiritual life. Now he found that as an unhappy man, he began to reap the bitter consequences of the wickedness he had tolerated. Moreover, the wealth that had been the cause of his quarrel with his uncle Abram was now the spoils of a merciless conqueror. We can easily become rich but lose ourselves in the process. In 2 Peter 2:7–8, we read that God "rescued Lot, a righteous man, who was distressed by the depraved conduct of the lawless (for that righteous man, living among them day after day, was tormented in his righteous soul by the lawless deeds he saw and heard)."

The Tragedy of Lot's Kidnapping Is Reported to Abram – 14:13–16

An escaped survivor made his way to where Abram was in the plain of Mamre, the Amorite. For the first time in Scripture, Abram is called

"Abram the Hebrew" (v. 13). The origin of this term, however, has divided scholars, with no consensus as yet. For instance, some refer to the etymology of the Hebrew word `ibri, which has the concept of one crossing or making passage from one point to another. Those who adopt this view object to deriving the name from Eber or Heber, the great-grandson of Shem, as there is no reason why his name should be used as an appellative, especially since five generations separate Abram and Eber. Moreover, it would seem that we are forced to such a patronymic usage of `ibri by Numbers 24:24, "And ships shall come from the coast of Chittim, and shall afflict Ashur, and shall afflict Eber." Here, "Ashur" refers to the sons of Ashur, i.e., the Assyrians. Therefore, "Eber" means the "sons of Eber" or simply "the Hebrews," which is exactly how the Greek Septuagint version renders this term. The Hebrews did not use "Eber" to refer to themselves; the term was used by non-Israelites. There was a group in the ancient Near East known as the Habiru or `Apiru. These people were on the edge of society and usually functioned as foreign slaves, mercenaries and the like. Whether the Israelites ever were part of this group, we do not know.

When Abram was told what had happened to Lot, the messenger found him at his dwelling near the great trees of Mamre, the Amorite, kinsman of Aner and Eshcol, Abram's allies. It is significant that at least two of Abram's allies gave their names to localities where they lived. Thus, Abram seems to be in league with the Amorites, as he makes agreements with both the Philistines (21:22–34) and the Hittites (ch. 23).

Abram called out his 318 "trained men" born in his household and quickly caught up with the invaders at the site of Dan, formerly called Laish (Genesis 14; Judges 18:7). The Hebrew word *hanikim* is used only once in the Old Testament (14:14), but it is found, in an Egyptian execration text from the nineteen century B.C.E. and in one fifteenth-century B.C.E. Taanach letter, where it means "armed supporters, or retainers."[2] The fact that the 318 men were born in Abram's house may indicate they were tied to their master by military alliances, or by actually being born in his household.

Abram split up his troops (i.e., he "divided them") as he and this group of 318 drew near to attack the four kings at night (v. 15). Thus, he stealthily hit these kings in a surprise raid, probably hitting them just before dawn. The four kings and their armies fled in disarray, but Abram pursued them all the way to Hobah, which is just north of the city of Damascus. Incidentally, the city of Hobah was the birthplace of Abram's servant Eliezer (Genesis 15:2).

Abram took back all that the kings had stolen, and he brought back his nephew Lot and all the other people (v. 16) to the king of Sodom.

Melchizedek, Priest-King of Salem – 14:17–24

As Abram returned from his routing of the four kings from Mesopotamia, the king of Sodom—who likely hid himself or escaped to a safe place when the battle was going on—now went out to meet Abram and Lot. He may have been one of several kings who turned out to welcome Abram home and hail his achievement and outstanding victory (v. 17). Interestingly enough, Abram was not like one of those attacking kings who, after victory, insisted on being recognized as master of the whole country. Abram was governed by different principles that led this servant of God.

King of Salem – Melchizedek

The place where the king of Sodom met Abram was the "Valley of Shaveh, which is the King's Valley" (v. 17b). This site is near Jerusalem, presumably on the north side of the city, for that is the direction they would hit as they came from Damascus. However, the Genesis Apocryphon (22:14) mentions this vale as being at Beth Hakkerem, or Ramat Rachel, which is two and half miles south of Jerusalem. It was from Jerusalem that Melchizedek, King of Salem, came (v. 18a; cf. Hebrews 7:2). Melchizedek's name means "king of righteousness."

Melchizedek Brought Bread and Wine

This priest-king of Salem brought bread and wine, apparently to refresh Abram, which seems to foreshadow the sacramental elements later used in the Lord's Supper or Eucharist. Surely it was at least a token of good-will, but it is difficult to be more precise. Some suggest Melchizedek and Abram had a covenant meal between them, but again we cannot be certain. To be sure, bread and wine was royal fare (cf. 1 Samuel 16:20), so this may merely be a portrayal of Melchizedek laying out a royal banquet for the returning conqueror. After all, he was a priest of El Elyon ("Most High God") and the first priest mentioned in the Bible.

Melchizedek Blessed Abram

No genealogy or background material is given for this priest-king, thereby making it possible for the writer of the book of Hebrews to say he was "without [a known] father or mother, without genealogy, without beginning of days or end of life, resembling the Son of God. He remains a priest forever" (Hebrews 7:3).

An act of blessing was one of the characteristic functions of a priest (v. 19), for Numbers 6:23, 27 and 1 Chronicles 23:13 affirm that it was a priest's duty "to bless in the name of the LORD." Therefore, such a blessing was more than merely extending a greeting of well-wishes; it had a prophetic note to it. This blessing acted as a seal of divine approval on what had been done for him in the victory Abram had just achieved. It may also be assumed that Melchizedek was already an acquaintance of Abram, for he probably knew that God had promised the land of Canaan to Abram, and that through him all the nations of the earth would be blessed. If these suppositions are correct, then this blessing from Melchizedek implied his devout acquaintance with the divine will of God, even if it were at the expense of his own worldly and ungodly countrymen.

Possessor of Heaven and Earth

Melchizedek likewise announced that the Lord had the sovereign right, as the one who possessed heaven and earth, to make whatever allotments on earth he pleased or saw fit to designate (v. 19)! The entirety of all that was in heaven and on earth belonged to the Lord himself.

Moreover, instead of launching into heaps of praise on Abram's valor or his skill in conducting a successful nighttime raid, Melchizedek instead raised praise to the God of Abram, who had been the One who actually conferred the victory on Abram's 318 men (v. 20).

Abram Gave Tithes of Everything He Recouped

It appears that while this exchange was going on between Melchizedek and Abram, the king of Sodom stood by and heard all that transpired, yet without taking any part or showing any interest in what was occurring. What was just then transpiring appears to have made no impression on him. He only cared for himself, even while he was witnessing what the author of Hebrews saw as an illustration of the calling of God on the life of Yeshua "after the order of Melchizedek" (Hebrews 5:10). This calling on Yeshua's life was so solemn and certain that it was ratified by an oath: "The LORD has sworn and will not repent. You are a Priest for ever after the order of Melchizedek" (Hebrews 7:21–28). "The eternal God will not go back on his word and his oath, for 'Eternity' is written on the brow of the High Priest." This Priesthood would be superior to all human orders of priests worldwide.

Abram Had Already Lifted Up His Hand

This is a Hebraism for Abram saying "I have sworn," stemming from the custom of raising one's right hand in the act of taking an oath. Thus, Abram had previously and decisively sworn in the presence of the Most High God what he would do regarding that part of the spoils that belonged to him. According to Arab custom, Abram would have been in his rights to take as his own the recovered goods and cattle, but he had made a decision long before encountering once again the king of Sodom, who evidently had managed to avoid the battle with the four kings. Apparently, Abram knew him as a vain-boasting, unprincipled ruler, so he purposely decided to stay clear of any hint of any type of obligation. The king may have already thrown some malicious barbs at Lot and his uncle on account of their faith in the Lord God! Furthermore, Abram had been blessed of God, so he did not need even a thread or a thong of a sandal from him (v. 23). The expression about refusing to take even a "thread" pointed to some kind of a fastener used to tie up one's hair or dress, while the "latchet" refers to a buckle on one's sandal that went over the top of the foot and between the big and little toes. The point was, Abram wasn't going to accept anything from this king, even something as small as a thread.

The king of Sodom thought Abram should give him all the persons he had rescued and he could keep all the goods and cattle, but Abram would have none of it except the share that belonged to his allies—Aner, Eschol, and Mamre (v. 24), mentioned in verse 13.

Conclusions

1. Lot, in some ways, had cast his lot in with the five kings of the Jordan Valley, so he deserved what was coming to them. He had found himself unequally yoked to the contemporary culture. It was time, therefore, for him to get a wake-up call from God.
2. Abram was able to secure the services of those who were living in the same area as he was living: Mamre, Eschol and Aner. Had they been won to the Gospel message in the meantime?
3. Abram's wealth required that he also raise up in his household 318 trained retainers to guard his herds, cattle and flocks. Had they been witnessed to as well?
4. The contrast between the king of Sodom and the king of Salem is very great.
5. As the book of Hebrews points out, Melchizedek is a wonderful illustration of Yeshua.

Questions for Thought or Discussion

1. Why was the angel unable to find even ten persons who were righteous in Sodom after Lot and his family had lived there? Did the two daughters of Lot have boyfriends?
2. Why was Abram so confident in the Lord's promise that he refused to take even one scrap of the loot from the King of Sodom?
3. Is Abram's association with Mamre, Eschol, and Aner different from the people Lot associated with in Sodom?
4. Should Lot and his family have hidden themselves, as the king of Sodom apparently did?

Lesson 5

The Abrahamic Covenant

Genesis 15:1–21

"And Abram believed the LORD, and he credited to him as righteousness." – Genesis 15:6

It is interesting that just as Genesis 14 ended with Abram's complete forfeiture of any claim to the plunder he had taken from the nighttime raid on the four kings from the east (vv. 22–24), Genesis 15 begins with God's assurance that he would make him rich by his "great reward" (v. 1c). But the Covenant God "cuts" with Abram in Genesis 15 is an even richer reward, for it sets forth God's plan for the ages and for the peoples of the world!

Four Striking Phrases

First of all, "the word of the LORD came to Abram in a vision" (v. 1). This is the fourth time in just four chapters where the word of the Lord was given to Abram (12:1–3; 12:7; 13:14–17; 15:1). It is this revelation from God that makes Abram a "prophet," for in these earlier days, prophets were known as "seers" (1 Samuel 9:9; 2 Samuel 24:11), just as a "prophecy" was called a "vision" in Isaiah 1:1. The Lord had promised in Numbers 12:6,

Where there are prophets of the LORD among you, I [will] reveal myself
to them in visions, I [will] speak to them in dreams.

Most of these visions and dreams came to the prophets in the evening hours, usually when the prophet was asleep, yet in other instances, the word from heaven was imparted so powerfully that the prophet had a strong understanding of the will and plan of God even during the daylight hours.

The divine message gives us the second striking phrase: "fear not" (v. 1b). Just as Abram had defeated the four eastern kings with what surely were far fewer troops than the kings he opposed, he might as a result of such over-balanced odds have worried for the moment that after his rout of these defeated troops would rally again later to reap vengeance on Abram and his lesser group of 318 trained retainers. But this would not happen, for our Lord, who watches over all the affairs of mortals, had declared it would not, so Abram should not fear.

The third striking phrase is "I am your shield," an obvious military metaphor (v. 1c), "your very great reward" (v. 1d). Our Lord promised to protect Abram and his seed and to reward him handsomely. Therefore, the Lord would add his reward to his protection. Even though nothing is said at this time about what the grounds of this reward were, nor the nature of this reward, the Lord had already given Abram his promise in Genesis 12, including inheriting the land of Canaan (v. 7), being blessed with numerous seed, and about being a source for blessing the whole world. Yet Abram had done nothing to earn or to merit such a reward, for as Romans 4:4–5 teaches:

> Now to anyone who works, their wages are not credited to them as a gift, but as an obligation. However, to anyone who does not work but trusts God who justifies the ungodly, their faith is credited as righteousness.

In the fourth and final striking phrase we meet the word "believe" for the first time in Scripture (v. 6). Abram's belief was counted as righteousness. In fact, there was no higher glory for any human than that he or she should count on the faithfulness and the reliability of God.

Abram's Question to God: How Will You Do This for Me? – 15:2–5

The literal rendering of the interrogative in verse 2 is, "How will you do this for me?" Abram had in mind one of God's promises in particular, for he had gone "childless" for 25 years now. He felt he would soon leave this world without any heirs, meaning the "steward of his house," Eliezer of Damascus, would be his heir and not any son born to him as the Lord had promised (v. 2)! It is noteworthy that Yeshua, in his parable of Lazarus[1] (the Greek form of "Eliezer") and the rich man in Luke 16:23, pictured Lazarus as safe in the "bosom of Abraham," which may have referred to Eliezer of Damascus.

Apparently, Abram's wife Sarai was barren (11:30). But despite Abram's adoption of Eliezer as his son, God announced that Eliezer would not be his heir. On the contrary, a son would issue from Abram and Sarai's union, and would be his heir (15:4). Abram had followed the customs of that day in adopting Eliezer, for according to the Nuzi documents,[2] an adopted servant could inherit the rights of a natural-born son when there were no sons born in that family, as was true at that time in Abram's family. That a son named Isaac was born later on changed all of this (21:2), thus making him the son "of promise" (Galatians 4:28), just as we who belong to

Messiah Yeshua are likewise called the "children of promise," as Paul declared in Galatians 4:21–31. Moreover, God promised that Abram and his offspring would be as numerous as the stars in the sky (Genesis 15:5), a promise that was repeated to Abram in Genesis 22:17 and was marveled at in Romans 4:18 and Hebrews 11:12.

Abram's Belief in the Coming Man of Promise – Genesis 15:6

Some believe that verse 6 suddenly changes syntax such that the narrator interrupts the narrative to emphasize the main idea of the section. But verse 6 opens with the Hebrew particle for the word "And," which indicates that the event being described in verses 2–5 is continuing. This fact, however, is hotly debated by several evangelical writers, and the NIV even leaves "And" untranslated. Nevertheless, I believe Abram finds here the strongest case for the fact that the object of his faith and his salvation was that coming promised "seed" who was to come from Adam's *own body.* That is why Acts 4:12 stresses that there is salvation in no other name under heaven by which we are saved than the name of Yeshua.

The central text in this debate, then, is Genesis 15:6, "[And] Abram believed the LORD, and he credited it [Abram's belief/trust in God's promise of the seed that would come from his body] to him as righteousness." However, Southern Baptist professor T. V. Farris contends:

> Verse 6, following immediately [vv. 2–5], would suggest that Abraham's faith was in response to the preceding promise [about God's provision of a "Seed"—which is what I am arguing here!]. The syntactical form of the verb "believed," however, *precludes* that interpretation. The precise nuance of the syntax formula used in this instance, the conjunction *vav* plus a perfect form of the [Hebrew] verb, is a matter of dispute among Hebrew grammarians.[3]

Likewise, Allen P. Ross, a Dallas Seminary professor, also wishes to separate verse 6 from verses 2–5 by asserting that the NIV leaves the conjunction rendered "And" untranslated to avoid the implication that verse 6 results or follows chronologically from verse 5. Ross adds:

> If the writer had wished to show that this verse followed the preceding in sequence, he would have used the normal structure for narrative sequence, *wa'amin,* and [then] "he believed"—as he did within the sentence to show that the reckoning followed the belief . . . "and [so then] he reckoned it."

> We must conclude that the narrator *did not wish to show sequence* between verses 5 and 6; rather, he wished to make a break with the narrative in order to supply this information about the faith of Abraham.[4]

Both analyses of Genesis 15:5–6 leave the context dangling by omitting the conjunction "And." Why did the writer of Genesis 6 include it then? Furthermore, not all Hebrew grammarians agree about the meaning of *vav* plus the Hebrew perfect conjugation used for the verb "to believe." By omitting the conjunction "and," they create another problem in order to solve the first problem. I conclude that verse 6 must be connected with verses 2–5, for that is how it is written.

Twenty-five years previous to this episode, when Abram had obeyed God and had left his homeland in Haran and journeyed to Canaan, chapters 12–14 never give any indication that he had already believed in God. But when Abram turned one hundred and Sarai ninety, Abram offered to help God fulfill his promise of an heir by adopting Eliezer of Damascus. God rejected such an offer of help and stated that he would still fulfill his promise of a son for this couple by himself. That promised son became the object of Abram's faith. He simply trusted what God had said, and the Lord counted it to him as righteous.

What shall we say, then, is "faith"? Is it "faithfulness" as most commentators say today? No, it is not, for the Hebrew word *'emunah* is more accurately translated here as "faith" or "trust," especially in this text, "And Abram believed the LORD, and he credited it to him as righteousness." Since there is no antecedent for the Hebrew feminine word "it" in Genesis 15:6, "it" then must refer back to the verb "believed," and to the corresponding feminine noun for that verb "to believe," which is *'emunah*, "belief." In fact, that is the precise noun Habakkuk chose to use in 2:4 to describe the person who, as contrasted with the arrogant, proud or "puffed-up" person was instead a "righteous" person "who shall live by faith."

But how does one become "righteous"? In this context, "righteousness" is not viewed as an ethical term but a religious one. It has a forensic or legal aspect in that it was a judge's term, whereby he pronounced a person innocent of all charges against him (cf. Exodus 23:7; 2 Kings 10:9; Job 13:18; Isaiah 5:23). Thus, the righteous person is not the one who has worked for a certain ethical status or one who showed his or her faithfulness;

it is God completely declaring that person "justified" and innocent of any charges of further guilt as a result of sins already committed.

The Abrahamic Covenant – 15:7–21

The opening statement in verse 7, "I am the LORD who brought you out of Ur of the Chaldeans," was later used in almost identical form as the opening statement for the Sinaitic Covenant with the Ten Commandments, which read, "I am the LORD your God, who brought you out of Egypt" (Exodus 20:2; Deuteronomy 5:6). Therefore, in this second revelation from God, no mention is made of a vision, but it was a word that apparently came directly from God. The reason God had brought Abraham out of Ur and then out of Haran was to give him the land of Canaan (v. 7b).

But Abram asked: "Sovereign LORD, "How can I know that I will gain possession of it?" (v. 8). Apparently, this was a request for a sign or some type of guarantee, perhaps the same sign as God would later on give to Gideon (Judges 6:17, 36–40) or the guarantee offered to King Hezekiah (2 Kings 20:8). The use of the name in the NIV of "Sovereign LORD" is used almost exclusively in Covenant Treaties made with Abraham and David, which reflects the unusual Hebrew form of the name as *Adonai Yahweh* (Genesis 15:2, 8; and in the Davidic Covenant in 2 Samuel 7:18, 19, 22, 28, 29).

Some time, then, must have passed, for as Abram watched over this scene of these cut-open animals, he was instructed to keep away the birds of prey. But he must have grown tired of shooing them away, for as the day went on and the sun began to set, Abram fell into a "deep sleep," perhaps exhausted by the day's events.

As the sun was setting, an opportunity for another spoken message came from God, for "a thick and dreadful darkness came over him" (v. 12b). Probably it indicated that in the midst of his deep sleep he felt a deep disturbance in his soul, something like a nightmare, or some deep dread or fear gripped him.

Abram was now told that his offspring would enter into the land of Egypt in the meantime and they would be oppressed for 400 years (vv. 13–16). However, when Jacob and his family would first enter Egypt, it would be under the direction of Jacob's son Joseph who had been made second only to Pharaoh in the land of Egypt. They were treated kindly at first, but in time, oppression and mistreatment began, which may have been the reason for the dread and fear that overcame Abram in connection with this new disclosure from God. Nevertheless, Israel would be miraculously and powerfully brought out of Egypt by the Lord, and they would come out with great possessions (v. 14). Israel would return to the land of Canaan "in the fourth generation," for up to the point when God was speaking to Abram prophetically, "the sin of the Amorites had not yet reached its full measure" (v. 16). The Lord graciously revealed to Abram that the promise would be fulfilled, but it would come through suffering, though Abram and his generation would not experience it.

When the sun had fully set and darkness had fallen over the land (v. 17a) on that momentous day of revelations from God, there "appeared" "a smoking fire pot with a blazing torch," or as the Hebrew says literally, "an oven of smoke and a torch of fire" (v. 17b). Today we think of modern ovens differently, but this "oven" (Hebrew *tannur*) seems to have been something like a large earthenware jar used for baking. We probably should not think of two separate objects here, such as the jar and the torch, but of a fire pot that held the burning torch inside of it as it now passed between the pieces. However, even more importantly, the smoke and the fire were symbols of the presence of God (Exodus 13:21; 19:18; 20:18).

The interpretation of this cultic act is communicated in verse 18, "On that day, the LORD made [literally, "cut"] a covenant with Abram.[5] A good parallel passage to help us understand this Covenant ceremony is Jeremiah 34:18, where the Lord spoke of the people passing between the divided or dismembered calf. In so doing, they were risking taking a curse on themselves and becoming just like the dismembered animals. The act of passing between the pieces said, in effect, "May God make me like this animal if I do not do what this covenant promised I would!" Therefore, when in Genesis God walked between the pieces, he took the responsibility for ensuring this covenant would be kept. Note that Abram did not walk between the pieces as well but was sound asleep off to the side.

As part of that "cut" (Hebrew *karat*) "covenant" (*berit*), the Lord gave to Abram the delineation of the boundaries in this document of a land grant. In 15:7 God had given Abram possession of the land, but had not specified any borders. Now the Lord will do so by beginning with the southern border at the Wadi El Arish (Hebrew *Nahar Mizraim*) all the way up to the great "river" of the "Euphrates" (Hebrew *Nahar Perat*) (v. 18b; Numbers 34:5). Some say the Lord meant the Nile River, or its eastern branch. If it meant the Wadi Egypt, it would depict a smaller river or brook that ran from about 30 miles south of the city of Gaza on the coast at a 45-degree southwestern angle to Ezion Geber on the Gulf of the Arabah. If we mean the Nile River, then this would mean all the land between the two great rivers of the Nile and the Euphrates would belong to Israel.

The names of ten foreign tribes are listed in verses 19–21. This is the longest list of pre-Israelite inhabitants of Canaan in the Old Testament. However, it must be an old list or at least an incomplete list, for it omits nations like the Philistines and the Moabites while it includes the little-known Kenites, Kenizzites, and Kadmonites. If Deuteronomy 7:1 is a complete list, only seven of the ten nations listed here were subjected.

Conclusions

1. God once again came to Abram with his word of revelation for the fourth time in four chapters.
2. Abram complained to the Lord that he still was without any of the promised children God had spoken to him.
3. God promised he would give him an heir and Abram believed God and the Lord counted his belief in this coming child as righteousness.
4. God "cut a Covenant" with Abram by walking down the aisle formed by the cut animals and taking the sole responsibility for keeping that promise to Abram.
5. God once again promised the land of Canaan to Abram and his offspring, but this time it defined its boundaries.

Questions for Thought or Discussion

1. Why did God reject Abram's adoption of Eliezer as his heir?
2. What was the "shield" and "great reward" God promised to Abram?
3. Why do some grammarians want to leave the "and" that verse 6 begins with untranslated? How would that affect the interpretation? What was the first time Abram believed God? Was it different from the object of our belief, i.e., Yeshua?
4. What boundaries did our Lord give for the land he promised to give to Abram and his descendants, and how does that match or differ from what Israel experienced so far?

Lesson 6

The Birth of Ishmael and the Sealing of the Covenant by Circumcision

Genesis 16:1–16; 17:1–27

> "You are the God who sees me . . .
> I have now seen the One who sees me." – Genesis 16:13

Abram had by now dwelt in the land of Canaan for ten years (16:3), and his wife Sarai had not as yet had any children God had promised to Abram (v. 1). This presented a situation where unbelief, especially on Sarai's part, could lead to some bad consequences—and it did!

Sarai Gives Her Egyptian Servant to Her Husband Abram – 16:2–3

Despite Abram's advanced age of 85, he did not appear to exhibit any impatience with the promise of God, as contrasted with Sarai's emotions. Sarai, now 75 years old, was not as sanguine about this delay, for she had still not yet become a mother. Perhaps her feelings as a wife also went out to her husband, especially for his happiness and esteem. So this, together with her own feelings about being barren as a wife, made her begin to vent her frustrations to her husband.

Sarai not only blamed her husband, but she also blamed the Lord, for in her view, "The LORD has kept me from having children" (v. 2). She expressed a distrust in the Lord, and instead of waiting for his timing and fulfillment of his promises, she developed a scheme by proposing to her husband Abram an alternate way to help the Lord accomplish what he had promised—a scheme that carried with it pernicious consequences.

She hoped that by doing evil, good might come of it. But instead, it laid a foundation for almost certain jealousies and future quarrels. She proposed to her husband: "Go sleep with my servant [Hagar]; perhaps I can build a family [or: 'obtain children'] through her" (v. 2c). In Hebrew, "obtain[ing] children" is literally "I may be built by her." The Hebrew word for a "son" is *ben*, perhaps derived from *banah*, "to build," as also the Hebrew word for "stone," '*aben*, may likewise be derived. Thus, "building" a family may be like building a house, "stone" by "stone," as "son" after "son" is added to the family. As Ruth 4:11 says, "the LORD make the woman like Rachel and like Leah, which two *did build the house* of Israel." Also, in Exodus 1:21, "And it came to pass, because the midwives feared God, that *he made houses*, i.e., he gave them children and extended their families into "houses."

Now both Abram and Sarai knew God had promised to give them a son (15:4), but Sarai remained barren (11:30). Such a proposal as sleeping with one's maid was practiced in the culture they lived in. The Nuzi Tablets, though coming from a later time of about 1500 B.C.E., once again provide us with the cultural analogy as they had already done so in Abram's temptation to adopt Eliezer of Damascus as an heir in Genesis 15:2–3 to help God fulfill his word! According to Nuzi law and the Code of Hammurabi, a man could produce a son by cohabiting with one of his servant girls in his house. However, according to Nuzi social customs, if a natural son was later born to that household, then the rights of this natural-born son would supersede the inheritance rights of any adopted son.

Unfortunately, Abram listened to Sarai (v. 2c). Hagar, an Egyptian bondwoman may have come into the family as one of those "maid-servants" presented to Abram by Pharaoh while Abram and Sarai were in Egypt during the famine (12:16). "Hagar" means "flight" or "fugitive."

Hagar was carefully called in this context the servant of Sarai, but she was not linked to Abraham, for the custom of those days was to keep male and female persons apart from each other. Likewise, Jacob's wives, Rachel and Leah, daughters of Laban, also had female bondservants (Genesis 30:3). It should be noted that the relationship between their mistress and themselves, however, was so intimate that any and all the children born to the bondservants were counted as the children that belonged to their mistress (Genesis 30:3, 6, 8). Thus, the children of the handmaidens were always counted in the number of children that belonged to the master (Exodus 21:4).

Interestingly enough, Abram heard God's promise and believed; it was enough for him that God had promised he would have an heir, even though he did not see it happening yet, nor was he told the means by which it would happen. But Sarai seems either weak in her faith or impatient for God to act.

Sarai Treats Hagar Harshly – 16:4–6

Sarai's plan worked, for when Abram slept with Hagar she became pregnant (v. 4). But what Sarai had not foreseen was that when Hagar conceived, she began to show disdain toward Sarai by flaunting her condition and contrasting her abilities over against those of her childless mistress (v. 4b). Sarai was not going to take this sitting down, so she began to reproach her husband Abram:

> "You are responsible for the wrong I am suffering. I put my servant in your arms, and now that she knows she is pregnant, she despises me. May the LORD judge between you and me." (16:5)

Poor Abram! Sarai's conduct was more than unreasonable, for she certainly was peevish and her anger ill-placed. First, she gave evil counsel to Abram, and then, instead of condemning her own conduct, she turned her resentment against her own husband. Moreover, she must have assumed her husband would not listen to her accusations, so she called on the Lord to judge between the two of them (v. 5d).

Abram seems to have approached this difficult situation with a spirit of meekness, kindness, and gentleness. Had he already learned that a soft answer turns away wrath? Anyhow, he did not take the path of accusing his wife, for it was, after all, her idea for him to commit polygamy! Instead, he merely noted that Hagar was under the guidance and oversight of his wife Sarai; therefore she was free to do with her as she pleased (v. 6). However, Scripture makes no comment on Abram's ill-judged compliance with his wife's plan, for clearly he shared some fault in this whole scheme. Was he all too happy to comply? Sarai carried out her plan, but in doing so, she decided to treat Hagar harshly as she put this pregnant girl in her place as a reply to Hagar's taunting her for her barrenness (v. 6d). As a result, Hagar "fled" from Abram's tent to escape Sarai's oppression.

An Angel of the Lord Appears to Hagar – 16:7–13

Hagar was able to flee from the face of her mistress Sarai, but not from God. The "angel of the LORD" appeared to Hagar, now a fugitive from Abram's tent, while she was resting near a spring in the desert. An "angel" is mentioned here for the first time in Scripture. The angel mentioned here, however, was more than an angel, for this person is called by Hagar "the LORD" [Hebrew *YHWH/Yahweh*] in verse 13. Moreover, he previously spoke in verse 10 in a manner that only the Lord himself could have, by promising an increase to her offspring to the degree that neither she nor anyone else would be able to count them in the future.[1] Thus, no one less than the eternal God himself was this angel addressing Hagar! The place where the angel met up with Hagar is said to be "beside the road to Shur," which according to Genesis 25:18 and 1 Samuel 15:7 was near the border of Egypt, indicating that Hagar was hoping to reach her homeland of Egypt.

The reference to the "spring" actually was a "well" where travelers stopped to refresh themselves. There it was that she heard someone addressing her by name and by her occupation (v. 8a). In calling her by her title of "Sarai's maid," instead of the "wife of Abram," the Lord may have been deliberately reminding Hagar of his view of marriage. The Lord also asked her rhetorically, "Where have you come from and where are you going?" Of course he knew, but he wanted her to acknowledge what she was doing.

Hagar responded, "I am running away from my mistress Sarai" (v. 8b). So the Lord directed her, "Go back to your mistress and submit yourself to her authority" (v. 9). The text here rendered "submit" is rendered in the Greek as "humble," much as 1 Peter 5:6 urges us to "humble ourselves under the mighty hand of God that he may lift us up." Sarai had indeed treated Hagar poorly and wrongly, but Hagar had done wrong by despising her mistress and by endangering the baby she was carrying in her womb. Only by going back to Sarai would she enjoy peace and happiness. Sarai's loss of the services may have been enough by now to also bring her to regret the way she had treated Hagar. Meanwhile, the solitude, heat and dangers of the wilderness might have brought some sense into Hagar's way of thinking as well.

God added to his command to return to Sarai this promise:

> I will increase your descendants so much that they will be too numerous to count. (16:10)

In the next chapter, the Lord added:

> As for Ishmael, I have heard you; I will surely bless him; I will make him fruitful and will greatly increase his numbers. He will be the father of twelve rulers, and I will make him a great nation. (17:20)

Naturally, what God had promised to Ishmael would also apply to his descendants as well. In fact, the Arab peoples have multiplied enormously over the ages as a result of this promise from God. And in a first instance in Scripture where a name is given to a mortal by divine direction prior to birth, Hagar is told to call him "Ishmael," which means "God has heard" her prayers (v. 10). Yet nowhere does Scripture say she had up to now called on the name of God in prayer. However, God's ear is ever open to what some call the "silent voice of affliction," which obviously Hagar shared extensively!

Ishmael is described as a "wild donkey of a man" (v. 12), "one in which his hand will be against everyone and everyone's hand against him." It would seem Ishmael and his offspring will be rude, fierce, uncultivated, and impatient of the restraints of civilized life, quite like a similar description in Job 11:12 or 24:5. By using such an unusual phrase, a forthright analogy was made between Hagar's future seed in its penchant for wildness and the actions of a wild ass (onager). Like the wild donkey, his seed would roam free over the hills of his country. Moreover, he would be in conflict with the people surrounding him and even with his own descendants (vv. 11–12).

Hagar Concludes That God Has Spoken to Her – 16:13–16

Now that Hagar had heard the Angel of the Lord, she concluded that God himself had spoken to her. She may have wondered how it was possible to have seen the Lord himself, and like Jacob did many years later (32:30), she could not figure out why she was still alive. For she directly affirmed: "You are the God who sees me. I have now seen the One who sees me" (v. 13). In memory of this event, she named the well *Beer-lahai-Roi*, meaning "The Well of the Living One who sees me" (v. 14).

So, why did the angel intercept her in the first place? He wanted to tell her these four things: (1) She should go back to her mistress Sarai and submit to her, (2) she would have loads of descendants, (3) God had "heard" her cry of affliction (16:11), and (4) she would bear a son named "Ishmael," whose name means "God hears" (same pun on this name is in 17:20). And so, Abram became the father of Ishmael at 86 years of age (vv. 15–16)! However, just as there had been antagonism between Sarai and Hagar, so there would be strife between Ishmael and his descendants and Sarai's son Isaac and his offspring. But that would all come in the future; meanwhile Abram rejoiced over the birth of his son Ishmael.

The Sealing of The Covenant by Circumcision – 17:1–27

Thirteen Years Later – 17:1

The promise of God had already been repeated in Genesis 12:2–3, 7; 13:14–16; and 15:5–7. Now, thirteen years after the Lord had last appeared to announce Ishmael's birth to Abram, the Lord appeared to Abram again in Genesis 17:1 and announced his name as "El Shaddai," which most English texts render as "God Almighty." God memorialized the event by stating his name as "El Shaddai."

The Name El Shaddai and The Lifestyle of Abram – 17:1–2

Recent study has tended to render "El Shaddai" as "God, the Mountain One," because a cuneiform word for mountain is *shaddu*. In its earlier form, this name was derived from the Hebrew *shad*, "breast." Hence, in this case "El Shaddai" would mean "God the Nourisher." It is the book of Job, however, that uses the divine name "El Shaddai" some 31 times. But this name was prominent in its Patriarchal usage, for as Exodus 6:3 notes:

> I appeared to Jacob as God Almighty [Hebrew *El Shaddai*], but by my name
> the LORD [Hebrew *YHWH/Yahweh*] I did not make myself known to them.

But the translation of "God Almighty" is also most appropriate for rendering "El Shaddai," since it focuses on the God who makes things happen by his mighty power and might, while the Hebrew name *YHWH/Yahweh*, usually rendered "LORD" (in small-caps), is God's covenant name.

After our Lord identified himself ("I am God Almighty"), he immediately stressed the need for Abram to "walk before him and [he] would be blameless" (literal translation). The imperative and noun, "be blameless" (Hebrew *wehyeh tamim*), are dependent on the preceding imperative "walk" (Hebrew *hithallek*). Thus, our Lord does not issue a command here, as if the covenant would be conditioned on Abram and his descendant's obedience to the covenant, which is what so many have incorrectly argued, but our Lord gives a consequence of an initial condition.[2] Thus it is better read: "If you walk before me, you will be blameless." The condition pertained to Abram's condition and not to the viability or authority of the covenant!

It is a matter of real concern when so many evangelical interpreters conclude that the meaning of this clause is this, as one commentator concluded: "Unlike the earlier covenant with Noah (9:8–17), this covenant was conditional on the obedience of Abram and his descendants (17:1, 9; 18:19; 22:18; 26:4–5; 30:15–20)."[3] But this Abrahamic Covenant was meant to be unconditional, for it was unilateral (i.e., one-sided), in that only God moved between the pieces and obligated only himself to maintain it.

Circumcision, the Sign of the Covenant – 17:3–16

In a second, much longer, speech to Abram, now called "Abraham" for the first time as God memorializes this name-change by promising a great number of descendants (17:5), this speech is divided into three sections, each beginning with the phrase "And God said" (17:3, 9, 15). Each of the three sections deals with one of the parties of the covenant: namely, the Lord (v. 4a), Abram (v. 9a), and Sarai (v. 15a). Moreover, each of the three sections is memorialized by a specific sign: the change of Abram's name to Abraham (v. 5), the circumcision of all males in the second section (vv. 10–14), and in the third section the change of Sarai's name to Sarah (v. 15).

The first section of the covenant (vv. 3b–8), which includes God's part in the covenant, he there makes two promises: lots of descendants (vv. 4–6) and eternal faithfulness (vv. 7–8). Abram's response to God's "appearance" (vv. 1, 3) was to cast himself down on the ground in humble worship. Abram was promised that he would "be the father of many nations" (v. 4). This must be viewed from both physical and spiritual bases, for "kings would come from [Abram]" (v. 6). Abram would also be a "father" to "children born, not of natural descent, nor of human decision, or a husband's will, but born of God" (John 1:13). To set apart this event in the memories of all, Abram's name was hereby changed from Abram to Abraham, signifying that as Abram meant "a great father," the name Abraham now meant "father of many nations" (v. 5). The promise that God would make him "fruitful" and "greatly increase his numbers" (v. 2) is a clear allusion to Genesis 1:28 in the creation narrative and repeated again in Genesis 9:1. This covenant would be an "eternal" or "everlasting" covenant as well (vv. 7, 8, 13, 19).

It is important to note that the mention of "kings" coming forth from Abraham not only included kings in the line of the Ishmaelites, as well as "kings" from Keturah's line (Genesis 25:1–4), but also the kings in the line of the Edomites too. Even more significantly, kings would come from Abram's line who would be in the royal line of David, which would produce the Messiah!

Abraham's part in the covenant (vv. 9–14) came as he was himself involved, his male children, and all in his household, in the rite of circumcision; every male at the age of eight days old had to be circumcised. Even if someone in his household was purchased with money, he had to be circumcised, for any who did not keep this rite would be excluded from the covenant (v. 14). This rite was not the entirety of the covenant by any means, but instead of circumcision being the whole of the covenant, it was only a sign of one's belonging to the covenant. Circumcision is found among the Ishmaelites, Edomites, Ammonites, Moabites, Phoenicians, and even among the Egyptians, as evidenced by some Egyptian mummies.

Sarai's part, in this third part of the covenant statement here, was to bear children (vv. 14–15), thus, she would be the mother to the nations and kings of peoples that would come from her (v. 16). To memorialize this event, her name would be changed to Sarah (v. 15), which meant "princess," since kings of peoples would come from her.

Abraham's Response to God's Promise – 17:17–22

When Abraham was told Sarah would bear him a son, his response was to fall on his face and to laugh (v. 17). There is considerable difference of opinion as to whether Abraham's attitude was one of unbelief or joyous amazement. Calvin and a number of conservative scholars take the latter interpretation; however, just as many conservative scholars seem to feel this revelation that Abraham would have a son when he was 100 years old and his wife Sarah was 90 was "incredible." According to this second group of interpreters, laughter here signaled unbelief, not joy. Some Jewish teachers, on the other hand, have argued that Abraham's laughter was only an expression of his modesty, for this was not an expression of Abraham's doubt, but one of being overwhelmed by God's announcement. Yet this must be separated from the time when Sarah "laughed," for in her doing so, she was rebuked by God for laughing (18:12–13). Can the absence of a divine rebuke to Abraham mean that Abraham's laughter did not express a lack of faith, as it did in Sarah's case, but one of joy and happiness? But if that is so, why did the author include the note about the Patriarch's laughing? Perhaps it was because the Hebrew expression "and he laughed" (Hebrew *wayitshaq*) foreshadowed the name "Isaac" (Hebrew *yitshaq*). At any rate, Abraham's laughter marked the remainder of the narrative about Isaac's birth, for as Sailhamer[4] notes, it is found in the following phrases:

Sarah laughed (18:12)
Lot's sons-in-law laughed (19:14)
All who hear of Sarah's giving birth to Isaac will laugh (21:6)
The sons of Hagar laughed (21:9b)

Isaac's own failure to trust God is uncovered when the Philistine king sees him laughing [caressing] with Rebekah (26:7)

God may have given Abraham a mild rebuke in 17:19 when he retorted: "Yes, but your wife Sarah will bear a son, and you will call him Isaac." Moreover, this covenant was not one that would endure only for that moment, but it was stated by the Lord that it would be "an everlasting covenant." If Abraham was worried about his thirteen-year-old son, "then what about Ishmael?" Yet God had heard Abraham's concern and God would certainly bless him, too (v. 20). God would make Ishmael fruitful and greatly increase his numbers—a fact that can easily be seen today to have been fulfilled very generously among the Arab peoples! Ishmael would be the father of twelve tribes and a great nation (v. 20). However, God's covenant with Isaac, Sarah's son, would surely be established by that very same time next year!

Then God left Abraham and "went up from him."

Circumcision Performed – 17: 23–27

Without delay, after the order to circumcise the flesh of the male foreskin had been divinely given, Abraham took Ishmael, who was now thirteen, along with all who were born in Abraham's household, or who had been bought with money, and he, as the circumciser (Hebrew *mohel*), circumcised all of them. Abraham also was circumcised at this same time, but we don't know by whom. Perhaps he performed it on himself.

Conclusions

1. Sarai designated her bondservant, Hagar, to sleep with Abram to conceive a child, but nowhere did God approve of such actions.
2. Abraham received another "appearance" from God as he once more confirmed the covenant he had already made with Abraham.
3. God announced his name as "El Shaddai," the Lord who was mighty in power and altogether trustworthy in performing what he had promised.
4. Abraham would be counted "blameless" if he "walked before God."
5. The Abrahamic Covenant is an unconditional and unilateral covenant in which God alone took on himself the responsibility for maintaining and fulfilling it.

6. The sign of this covenant was circumcision just as the sign that God would never flood the earth again was the rainbow.

Questions for Thought or Discussion

1. Did Abraham's "laughter" indicate a lack of faith, or was it a sign of joy and happiness?
2. If God had made the Abrahamic Covenant dependent on Abraham's obedience, what effect would that have on the viability of the covenant for the ages to come?
3. How are the promises made to Ishmael the same or different from those made to Abraham? How will this make a difference in the future?
4. What order do you detect in the divine speech to Abraham in Genesis 17:3b–16? What does this say about the character of God?

Lesson 7

Three Men Visit Abraham With News About Sarah's Future Pregnancy and Sodom and Gomorrah's Destruction

Genesis 18:1–33

"Is anything too hard for the LORD?" – Genesis 18:14a
"Will not the Judge of all the earth do [what is] right?" – Genesis 18:25c

One hot afternoon, the LORD appeared, along with two other men, to Abraham near the "great trees of Mamre," oak trees that were not too far from Hebron (Genesis 13:18), while he was sitting in the shade of the entrance to his tent (18:1). Abraham, however, felt he must show hospitality to these three strangers, much as Hebrews 13:2 will later teach, "Do not neglect to show hospitality to strangers, for by this some have entertained angels without knowing it." Indeed, that was especially true in this situation.

The Case for Abraham and Sarai Confronting a Christophany – 18:1–8

As Abraham looked up, lo and behold he saw three men standing nearby. Some interpreters claim these three were a manifestation of the Christian Trinity, but two of them, who went on to Sodom, are specifically called "men."

But who was the third one in this trio of visitors? A comparison of Genesis 18:1, 16; 19:10, 12, 16 strongly suggests that this was none other than a manifestation of the second person of the Tri-unity, the Son of God himself, who had appeared to Abraham in the flesh prior to his incarnation as Yeshua. At first Abraham just saw these three men as mere human travelers passing by who needed rest and refreshment, as do many in that part of the world.

In Genesis 18:3, it is somewhat unusual that this patriarch addressed these three men by a singular title, "If I have found favor in your eyes, my lord, do not pass your servant by." Some mistakenly believe Abraham instantly recognized one of the men as the Lord himself, and some rabbinical scholars also thought this singular form of "my lord" must have signaled deity, so they placed vowel letters (thereby lengthening the final diphthong in the Hebrew word `adonay)[1] under the word "lord" to indicate deity, but Abraham would not have offered a meal if he had thought he was speaking to God himself. Abraham must have thought he was addressing the leader of the group.

Abraham continued his hospitable offer by using the plural form of address to all three. He ordered that water be brought to wash his guests' feet, a real priority for travelers in the Near East who walked the dusty paths shod only with sandals. He also invited them to come and rest under the shade of the tree that no doubt enveloped his tent and environs. Then Abraham insisted they have something to eat so they would be refreshed for the rest of their journey (vv. 3–5a). And to this invitation, the three visitors merely said, "Very well, do as you say" (v. 5b).

Abraham hurried into the tent to urge Sarah to hastily bake some bread (v. 6). The bread of those times was shaped in the form of flat cakes, much like pita bread, for they were usually made of fine flour baked on hot stones. Then he personally ran to select from his herd a "choice, tender calf" and asked his servant to quickly prepare it (v. 7). Meanwhile the three strangers must have rested while they waited, for there were no microwave ovens in that day. To this fare, Abraham added some "curds and milk" (v. 8a). When it was ready, Abraham served it to the strangers while he stood nearby under that same oak tree, ready to care for their every need (v. 8b).

Today, we as interpreters may question that if these men were supernatural beings, how could they partake of physical food? Some have tried to solve this by saying the three did merely pretended to partake of the food, but Scripture does not support such an interpretation. Anyway, Yeshua apparently ate fish with his disciples by the Sea of Galilee (John 21:10–14) after his resurrection.

The Promise of a Son Born to Abraham and Sarah – 18:9–15

After the guests had eaten from Abraham's provisions, they asked, "Where is your wife Sarah?" (v. 9) This must have increased Abraham's realization that he had not entertained ordinary guests, for they knew her name. They must have come to announce a heavenly message for her, for they seemed to know her barrenness without anyone telling them (v. 10).

Sarah was eavesdropping on the men's conversation from behind the tent, so when she heard this declaration that by this same time next year she would have a son, she just laughed—at least just to herself (vv. 10–12). Suddenly the text no longer treats one of the strangers as just an Eastern traveler, but it was the "LORD" who had made this prediction, and who wanted to know why Sarah had laughed (v. 13). God's question to Sarah—and to all of us studying this passage—is this: "Is anything too hard for the Lord?" (v. 14) The Hebrew word for "too hard" is *pele`*; the verb's meaning is "to be too miraculous, too difficult, too hard, too wonderful." The basic meaning of the verb form of this noun is "to be wonderful" or "to cause something wonderful to happen." Victor P. Hamilton describes this word *pele`* thus:

> "Preponderantly both the verb and the substantive refer to the acts of God, designating either cosmic wonders or historical achievements on behalf of Israel. . . . As such, it awakens astonishment in man. Thus, the real importance of the miraculous for faith is—not in its material factuality, but in its evidential character."[2]

Sarah, like many of us, denied she had laughed (v. 15), obviously forgetting what a powerful God he is. Did not an angel have to remind the Virgin Mary of the same truth concerning her own pregnancy and the pregnancy of her relative Elizabeth: "Nothing will be impossible with God" (Luke 1:37)? Of course, from a human point of view, it seems impossible, as it did to Mary, that a virgin could conceive, but that conclusion fails to take into account the mighty power of God. What was true in the physical realm was also true in the spiritual realm, for when the disciples heard Yeshua's assertion of how hard it was for rich men to go to heaven, they wanted to know, "Who then can be saved?" Yeshua, however, looked these disciples straight in the face and answered, "With human beings this is impossible, but with God all things are possible" (Matthew 19:25–26).

The full majesty of God's power becomes evident as the Lord further questions Abraham, "Why did Sarah laugh?" Did she really say, "Will I really have a child now that I am old?" Of course she did, for the Lord knew Sarah had laughed inwardly as she considered the whole thing to impossible. Sarah was afraid, but she also lacked faith in God, so she denied having laughed. The word "laughter" is mentioned in Abraham's laughter in Genesis 17:17; and in Sarah's in 21:6) in order to focus on the name given to "Isaac," which means "he laughs." But even more importantly, a new reminder is given to the previous promise that Abraham and Sarah would have a son at this same time the following year.

Sodom Is Now the Concern for Justice – Genesis 18:16–21

As the three men got up to leave, they looked down to Sodom, as Abraham walked along with them and saw them on their way (18:16). The writer of this Scripture wanted to place together with the scene in verses 1–15 this additional scene in which the three men met with Abraham. It also is apparent that Abraham had since realized that his three visitors were most-distinguished guests—one of them was no less than God himself!

Thus, as a good Eastern host, Abraham extended the usual courtesy of accompanying his guests as they went on their way. But the writer also skillfully prepares us for the next narrative that will come in Genesis 19, noting in 18:16 that the visitors "looked down toward Sodom." Our heads turn along with the visitors' as they gaze upon the doomed city of Sodom.

We are not given any indication as to how far Abraham walked with the three men. Tradition, however, claims that this exchange among the four of them took place at a site northeast of Hebron, on the highest point in the hills of Judea, from where there is a great view of the Dead Sea if one looks through a cut in the mountains. Accordingly, then, the narrative about the birth of Isaac is dropped, and not mentioned again until chapter 21.

All of a sudden, the Lord interjected a question into the conversation, "Shall I hide from Abraham what I am about to do?" But to whom did he speak these words? The other two men? The text does not indicate to whom he addressed this question. It could not be to Abraham; his name was part of the question! Regardless of who he was speaking to, God announced why he was offering this special word to Abraham at this time. The reason was because Abraham had a special relationship to the Lord as already described in Genesis 12:2–3. The Genesis 18:18–19 text explains:

> Abraham will surely become a great and powerful nation, and all the nations on earth will be blessed through him. For I have chosen him, so that he will direct his children and his household after him to keep the way of the LORD by doing what is right and just, so that the LORD will bring about for Abraham what he has promised him.

These words reveal both the Lord's inner motivation and the reason for his decision to openly disclose to Abraham what he was about to do. We are thereby led into even the very thought-processes of our Lord. But we are also told, more importantly, that he hasn't forgotten his original promise to make Abraham a "great nation" and a nation that will by the avenue and means of blessing all the nations on the face of the earth (12:3b).

What is more, verse 19 expanded on what the Lord had meant in 17:1 when he advised Abraham, "Walk before me and be blameless." In a most amazing way, we are given an unusual piece of divine reflection on what has transpired in the life of Abraham up to this point in the narrative of Genesis.[3] Now, for the first time, we are told of Abraham's personal selection and election: "I have chosen him" (Hebrew *yeda*—a word that in other contexts means "to know" or "take notice of").

We are now told exactly the purpose of God's choosing Abraham, and it now exceeds what we have been told so far: "to keep the way of the LORD" (v. 19b). This is what the Lord had in view: that Abraham and his descendants would do "what is right and just" (v. 19c). Only when Abraham and his descendants have done what was right and just would "the LORD bring about for Abraham what he has promised" (v. 19d). Such a concept of internalized obedience comes very close to meaning what the New Covenant will make clear when it promises: "I will put my law in their minds and write it on their hearts" (Jeremiah 31:33); "The LORD your God will circumcise your hearts and the hearts of your descendants, so that you may love him with all your heart and all your soul, and live" (Deuteronomy 30:6).

Some interpreters, however, realizing that verses 17–19 were not addressed to Abraham, pose the alternate view that the Lord was merely thinking out loud about what he is now going to do. However, there is no disagreement on verses 20–21, for there all agree that Abraham is indeed addressed directly this time, for now the Lord will answer the question he had, according to the discussion we just posed, mused on in verse 17: "Shall I hide from Abraham what I am about to do?" Yes, the Lord will tell Abraham what he is about to do; after all, Abraham was God's "friend" as Scripture states three times (2 Chronicles 20:7; Isaiah 41:8; James 2:23), and good friends often share otherwise closely guarded secrets. Moreover, Abraham was also called a "prophet" (Genesis 20:7), and since God does nothing without telling his plans to his servants the prophets (Amos 3:7), the answer to God's question is a foregone conclusion!

Abraham Intercedes for Sodom – 18:22–33 [4]

After this conversation between Abraham and the three men, two of them turned away (cf. 19:1) and went on toward Sodom; however, the Lord did not go on toward Sodom. Instead, he stayed there, standing in front of Abraham. There is good evidence that the Hebrew text originally did read, "YHWH/Yahweh [the LORD] stood before Abraham" (v. 22). The Hebrew scribes, known as the Masoretes, preserved a list of eighteen times[5] where the most-ancient Hebrew text was deliberately changed by them, for in their pietistic way, it was unthinkable that the Shekinah glory would actually stand there as if waiting on a mortal such as Abraham to make his requests known to the Lord. Therefore, the scribes, in rare instance, changed the text to the way it reads today in our English translations, "Abraham [remained there] standing in front of the Lord." These eighteen textual "corrections" are known in Hebrew as *tiqqune sopherim*, "emendations by the scribes." A similar situation can be found in 1 Samuel 3:10, where the text says that after the Lord had called Samuel for the third time, "The LORD came and stood there, calling as at other times." Imagine, the high, awesome and holy God standing in front of the likes of us, waiting to hear our requests. Awesome!

The wickedness of these cities of the plain was already well-known, as Genesis 13:13 pointed out. So terrible was the sin of Sodom and Gomorrah that those cities' wickedness became proverbial (e.g., Ezekiel 16:49, 50). The Lord was going "to go down" to inspect the wickedness and reason for the "outcry" that had come up to him from these cities (18:20, 21), just as he went down to inspect what was going on as the Tower of Babel was being constructed (Genesis 11:5).

Abraham never once doubted the justice and righteousness of the actions the Lord had to take in the case of these cities, clearly affirming: "Will not the Judge of all the [whole] earth do [what is] right?" (18:25d) Abraham must have been aware of what was by then rather-public knowledge that the wickedness of this place was so great that it was deserving of God's judgment. But Abraham hoped there were some righteous persons in those cities for whom God might show extended mercy—at least for the sake of his nephew Lot, who had moved there.

In light of Abraham's understanding of who God was and what authority he possessed, this "friend of God" dared a few questions. First he asked: "Will you sweep away the righteous with the wicked? (18:23b). Surely, Abraham contended, the Lord would differentiate between the guilty perpetrators of evil and the innocent righteous persons living in those cities. But Abraham had a second question. "What if there were fifty righteous people in the city? Will you really sweep it away and not spare the place for the sake of the fifty righteous people in it?" (18:24) As if to remind God of his general character, Abraham added: "Far be it from you to do such a thing—to kill the righteous with the wicked, treating the righteous and the wicked alike. Far be it from you!" (18:25) Talk about leading the witness! It almost seems as if for the moment that Abraham is slipping into a teaching mode, offering to help our omniscient God with a decision!

At first Abraham thought there might be fifty such persons left in Sodom. But Abraham must have mused, *Come to think of it, Sodom is one awfully wicked place—perhaps there are not even fifty righteous people in that den of iniquity.* Even though the Lord had graciously acceded to his number of fifty, Abraham began one of the boldest intercessory prayers in the Bible and quickly reduced the number of the righteous in Sodom to save the city from destruction to forty-five (v. 27). It is true that he did try to present his bold request in a humble way ("though I am nothing but dust and ashes"), yet he still asked if God would spare Sodom where Lot and his family lived (v. 28).

Having gained this much so far, Abraham thought he had better try for forty. Once again, God accepted his "friend's" new request (v. 29). But with what might have appeared to the Lord as a bit of chutzpah, Abraham again prefaced his lowering the request to thirty by asking the Lord "not to be angry" with him (v. 30). So Abraham pleaded for Sodom on the hopes that there were thirty righteous souls!

Abraham was now on a roll, for he had helped his nephew Lot and the city of Sodom by reducing the number by twenty. So he gently began by asking the Lord, no doubt with his brow knit and perhaps in a somewhat softer voice, what about twenty persons. Would that be enough to save a city? (v. 31)

Emboldened by his success of already getting thirty fewer people off the original request, Abraham—perhaps exhibiting a good bit of humble pie—asked: "May the LORD not be angry, but let me speak just once more. What if only ten can be found there?" (v. 32) The Lord answered, "For the sake of ten, I will not destroy it" (v. 32b). Wow. That few. How many people lived in these cities at that time? Perhaps ten or fifteen thousand?

"When the LORD had finished speaking with Abraham, he left, and Abraham returned home" to Hebron the oaks of Mamre (v. 33). Why did Abraham stop at ten? Perhaps he was doing some mental arithmetic and calculated that Lot and his wife, along with their two unmarried daughters, totaled four. Perhaps the girls had two boyfriends who attended their Bible study in that city and were also believers, which would make six. However, the two future sons-in-law refused to heed the warning, for they thought Lot joked with them (19:14). This meant there were only four righteous, not ten! Per Jewish tradition, ten men are needed to form a *minyan* (quorum) for prayer. This practice is based in part on this account and is still followed in observant synagogues.

This chapter of Genesis has some astounding teaching. It sets forth the standard that families, towns, cities, counties, and countries can be rescued from imminent danger of the judgment of God for accumulated wickedness and sin if the prayer of the righteous goes up to him and there are even as few as ten believers in that place! This is very similar to what Jeremiah discovered in the Potter's House message that was given to him (Jeremiah 18:7–1).

> "If at any time I announce that a nation or a kingdom is to be uprooted, torn down and destroyed, and if that nation I warned repents of its evil, then I will relent and not inflict on it the disaster I had planned. And if at any time I announce that a nation or a kingdom is to be built up and planted, and it does evil in my sight and does not obey me, then I will reconsider the good I had intended to do to it."

Conclusions

1. The pre-incarnate Son of God, along with two angels, visited Abraham in Hebron to personally announce that Sarah and Abraham would have a son.
2. Sarah learned that "nothing is too hard for God."
3. Sarah's laughing, even though it was an inward laugh, was known by God and indicated her lack of trust in the mighty power of God.
4. God did not hide from his "friend" Abraham what he was about to do, for Abraham also was a "prophet." God would do nothing without revealing to his prophets what it was he was going to do.
5. The boldest prayer in the Bible is the one where Abraham intercedes for Sodom and his nephew Lot.
6. Lot and Abraham found out that "the Judge of the whole earth will do what is right."

Questions for Thought or Discussion

1. What is the lesson of hospitality that the narrative of the three men visiting Abraham teach us? How good are we as believers at practicing hospitality?
2. Do supernatural beings also eat of our food? Consider that Abraham prepared a calf as part of their meal. What does this say to vegans?
3. In what sense does God still not do anything in his plan for the nations and for the world unless he reveals it to his prophets? Are there prophets in our modern times as well?
4. How powerful is the prayer of one person offering intercessory prayer on behalf of a people, a nation, or a crisis?

Lesson 8

The Destruction of Sodom and Gomorrah and the Incest With Lot's Daughters

Genesis 19:1–38

"So when God destroyed the cities of the plain, he remembered Abraham and he brought Lot out of the catastrophe . . ." – Genesis 19:29

Two Angels Meet Lot at the Gate of Sodom – 19:1–14

In verse 1, the word "angels" is used to describe two of the three persons who had visited Abraham in Genesis 18, but in 19:10, 12, and 16 they are called "men" (Hebrew *ha'nashim*). The angels arrive in the open area at the city gate of Sodom as evening begins to fall. They find Lot seated in the city square. The city gate was where the citizens assembled, as in other city gates of this period—to converse on matters of public affairs, to hold courts of justice, and to set up open markets. Some commentators understand Lot's sitting in the gate to indicate that he was carrying out the task of a magistrate as one of the city elders. If so, Lot might have been an older man by this time and a resident of Sodom, perhaps one who had attained some long-term standing among similar elders in the gate of Sodom.

When Lot saw the two strangers arrive in the city square, he rose to meet them and bowed graciously before them (v. 1b). Just like Abraham, Lot immediately offered them hospitality, since there were no inns in the Eastern countries at this time. At first, the visitors refused Lot's offer of hospitality in his home, which was the normal mark of civility as part of Near Eastern hospitality. However, their refusal was a mark of common Near Eastern etiquette. The angels acted as if it were safe for them to lodge there in the open square or the city's streets, even though they surely knew such was not the case, given the city's wicked reputation. This gave Lot the further opportunity to show his concern for their welfare by insisting they stay at his house.

Lot wouldn't take no for an answer. He insisted they accept his offer to wash their feet and stay the night, then continue on their way early in the morning (v. 3). So they finally agreed and entered his house. Lot made a feast for them, as was customary in such situations. He baked "unleavened bread" (the same kind of bread Israel would eat during the Passover meal; see Exodus 12:8), for there was no time to bake bread with leaven; by this time Sodom's wickedness had reached epic proportions. The news of the arrival of strangers to the city must have spread like wildfire, so all the men of the city gathered outside Lot's house.

The citizens of Sodom gathered with the obvious intent of sexually abusing these visitors in their seeking to satisfy their homosexual lusts. The men of Sodom circled the house and began calling out to Lot: "Where are the men who came to you tonight? Bring them out to us so that we may know them" (v. 5).

An enormous amount of debate in our day has surrounded "to know" in this context. The Hebrew verb *yada`*, "to know," appears 1058 times in Scripture, of which fifteen refer to sexual knowledge. Of the fifteen references, heterosexual intercourse observed in marriage is in view except for two of the fifteen instances—Genesis 19:5 and Judges 19:22. Incidentally, Hebrew shares with other Semitic languages this same connotation of sexual knowledge for the word "know," as seen, for example, in the Code of Hammurabi, law #130.[1]

Lot tried to prevent the Sodomites from the wicked goal they had purposed for his two guests. Lot went out to the street and closed the door to his place behind him (v. 6). He pleaded with the aroused male crowd not to violate the hospitality he had offered his visitors. Lot's high regard for the rites of hospitality are indeed commendable, but when he offered his two daughters instead, he proposed to substitute one evil for another evil as a means of protecting his guests—a method neither Scripture nor morality (nor a father's responsibility) would permit! It is extremely difficult to understand Lot's outrageous proposal or to try to justify his behavior. Surely, this was a huge moral lapse in Lot's character. Even though this was surely an extremely difficult and dangerous situation for Lot and his family, his action in this critical moment may have indicated the moral drift in some of Lot's earlier thinking when he chose "to pitch his tents near Sodom" (13:12).

It is true, of course, that God . . .

> rescued Lot, a righteous man, living among [the ungodly] by the depraved conduct of the lawless (for that righteous man, living among them day after day, was tormented in his righteous soul by the lawless deeds he saw and heard). (2 Peter 2:7–8)

Lot's twisted reasoning in offering his own daughters showed a serious moral failing—even if he would be called a "righteous man" in the New Testament! And this street encounter between Lot and the men of Sodom also showed why there was such an "outcry" to God about the depth to which that culture had sunk (18:20)! There comes a time when enough is enough!

But there was no stopping these savage Sodomites, who angrily ordered Lot to "get out of our way," or they would deal worse with him than with his two guests (v. 9). Moreover, they chorused a further complaint: "This fellow came here as a foreigner, and now he wants to play the judge!" (v. 9b) With such speeches they also pressed against Lot all the harder, hoping to break down the door to his house to reach his guests (v. 9c).

Suddenly, the angels inside the house reached out, pulled Lot back in and slammed the door shut (v. 10). Then they struck the men with "blindness." The Hebrew word used here for "blindness" appears only one other time in the Bible—2 Kings 6:18. In the days of the prophet Elisha, the king of Syria wanted Elisha captured and taken captive, for he was giving otherwise-inaccessible information to the king of Israel about all the troop movements of the Syrian army—in fact, even what the Syrian king was saying in his bedroom, the prophet could disclose to the king of Israel! So God sent through Elisha the same kind of confused vision to the Syrian army that the angelic beings cast over the men of Sodom. All the men, young and old, were impaired in their vision, so no matter how much they tried, they could not find the door they wanted so badly to burst down (v. 11). They wanted to "know" the visitors who had come to town but did not even "know" where the door to the house was! These perverts were stopped by this "miracle" of "blindness," and so they must have left the scene as Lot with his family and two guests finally were able to spend the night in peace and security.

It was now time for the angels to announce their mission (vv. 12–13). They had come to destroy the cities of Sodom and of the Plain. The "outcry" against this city had been too great in the ears of the Lord (v. 13). Accordingly, the two angels asked, "Do you have anyone else here—sons-in-law, sons, or daughters, or anyone else in the city who belongs to you?" (v. 13) These were supernatural beings, but they were not omniscient as the Lord was, so they had to inquire about those connected with Lot!

So, Lot went out into the city, apparently after the mob had dispersed, and spoke with his sons-in-law, "who were pledged to marry his daughters" (v. 14). The Hebrew words rendered in the NIV as "were pledged," *loqehay benotayv*, meant literally "the takers" of his daughters. The Greek version of this text uses the past tense—"who *had taken*" his daughters in marriage. These sons-in-law apparently thought Lot was "joking" about the destruction of Sodom. The Hebrew word here translated as "joking," *tsahaq*, is the same word used to describe Sarah's incredulous laughter 18:12, 13, 15. They too thought the news about a pending destruction was ludicrous and Lot was not to be taken seriously. Why? Perhaps because Sodom had enormously thick walls, so who or what could penetrate that?

Lot Requests to Go to Zoar Instead of to the Mountains – 19:15

As dawn broke with the light of a new day, the two angels were doing their best to hurry Lot, his wife and two daughters out of the city, lest they "be swept away when the city [was] punished" (v. 15). The clause announcing that the city would "be swept away" (vv. 15, 17) recalls the prayer of Abraham in which he asked God: "Will you sweep away the righteous with the wicked?" (18:23) Lot hesitated—not because he disbelieved the word of God, but perhaps because he found it difficult to leave everything he had accumulated in those years of herding his flock in that rich and fertile valley. The men grabbed his hand, and those of his wife and daughters, as they escorted them out of Sodom to a place of safety (v. 16). But it is important to note that God delivered them from Sodom not because of Lot's righteousness, as Abraham had prayed, but because "the LORD was merciful to them" (v. 16c). Lot may have been a righteous man, but the text emphasizes God's compassion; Lot had found "favor" and "kindness" from God!

Once they were outside the city walls, one of the angels commanded them: "Flee for your lives! Don't look back and don't stop anywhere in the plain! Flee to the mountains, or you will be swept away!" (v. 17) Despite the urgency of using every minute for the flight ahead, Lot balked; in his view there was not enough time to reach the mountains before the catastrophe broke, so he asked if he could go to a small village nearby instead. The town, he argued, was a "little" town. So even though it was one of the five towns that were under God's judgment, could he spare this town and allow Lot to go there instead of to the mountains (v. 20)? Once more, God acceded to his request, and the town formerly known as "Bela" (Genesis 14:2) was renamed "Zoar," meaning "little, small," based on Lot's remark (v. 20). "Very well," answered the Lord, but get going quickly, "because I cannot do anything until you reach it" (v. 22). God's restraint was not due to an inability to act but rather the necessary delay to fulfill his promise. But Lot's wife disobeyed and looked back, and she "became a pillar of salt" (v. 26). Why she disobeyed is not told to us, but she apparently longed for all that was now going to go up in smoke![2]

This was the last day the city of Sodom ever saw the light of day, for as the sun was coming up on Sodom that final day as Lot and family reached Zoar (v. 23), judgment struck Sodom and the other three cities. "Then the LORD rained down burning Sulphur on Sodom and Gomorrah" (v. 24).

The Doomed Cities of Sodom and Gomorrah – 19:16–29

It appears that the infamous cities of Sodom and Gomorrah have now been found.[3] Evangelical professor Bryant G. Wood laid out the evidence for this claim in 2008.[4] These two "Cities of Plain," which were "well-watered," extended as far south as Zoar (Genesis 13:10). The Hebrew words for "well-watered" are *kullah*, an intensive form of the verb meaning "to be complete," and *masqeh*, meaning "to give to drink, to irrigate." No wonder, then, at least these two cities grew barley, wheat, grapes, figs, lentils, and flax along with chickpeas, peas, broad beans, dates, and olives.

When the two angels came to Sodom, they found Lot sitting in the city gate (v. 19:1), but this city likely was the site of Bab edh-Dhra, meaning "gate of the arm." Sodom and Numeira were two towns southeast of the Dead Sea, existing between about 3300 and 900 B.C.E. To locate these towns, the most important source is the Madaba Map, a mosaic map on the floor of a church in Jordan. The map depicts the small town of Zoar, located south of the Dead Sea, as well as the "Sanctuary of St. Lot," a church built in memory of Lot, at the edge of the mountains just east of Zoar. The ruins of this sanctuary have been discovered, built in front of a cave, thought to be the one Lot and his daughters later resorted to.

North of this site on the eastern shores of the Dead Sea is Numeira, whose Arabic name may preserve the name "Gomorrah."

If Bab edh-Dra is indeed Sodom, then it was a town of 9–10 acres with a massive wall 23 feet wide, and made of stone and mud bricks, holding a population of 600 to 1200. The residents of Numeira apparently buried their dead in the large cemeteries of Bab edh-Dra. Remember, this plain had rather large deposits of asphalt (tar pits; Genesis 14:10), which could have added to the conflagration from the material that fell from heaven. What rained down is called in Hebrew *goprit*, meaning "brimstone," probably from the Akkadian *ki/ubritu*, meaning a sulphurous oil (black sulphur) along with "fire." Thus, the cities of the Plain, except for Zoar, were burned up. No wonder, then, that when Abraham looked down on the conflagration of these cities, he saw what was "like smoke from a furnace" rising from the Plain. The Hebrew word used for "furnace" (*kibshan*), is a pottery kiln. Even the Hebrew word used for "smoke" is not the usual word; it is a rather "thick smoke" found also in sacrifices. All of this data suggests there was something going on here that was supernatural, not a run-of-the-mill city fire. So the Lord destroyed these cities of the Plain, but he rescued Lot, because the Lord remembered Abraham's intercession on Lot's behalf.

Lot's Incest With His Daughters – 19:30–38

Lot decided not to stay in Zoar; he was afraid to do so for some reason (v. 30), so he later on moved to the hills. He took up residence in a cave, which must have been a real come-down for him after he had lived the high-life in Sodom. Lot's two daughters, who had remained with him, began to fear their isolation would mean they would not be able to find any male companionship resulting in a marriage and the joy of raising a family. Ironically, in his drunkenness, Lot himself carries out the shameful act he had proposed to the men of Sodom (19:8) as he lies with his own daughters. In doing so, he repeats the final days of Noah, after God had saved him from the Flood (Genesis 9:20–27).

Then, sometime later, Lot's older daughter suggested they take action to remedy their childless condition. She laid out the case for her younger sister (v. 31) as she sized up the situation thus:

> "Our father is old, and there is no man around here to give us children—as
> is the custom all over the earth. Let's get our father to drink wine and then
> sleep with him and preserve our family line through our father." (31b–32)

They must have agreed on this plan, for that very night they got their father drunk. The older daughter went in and laid down with Lot, but he apparently was unaware of when she came to lie down or when she got up (v. 33). However, she did get pregnant. The next day, the older one urged her sister to take her turn sleeping with her father, so once again they got their father drunk with wine, and the younger daughter repeated her sister's actions of the previous night (vv. 34–35). In this way, Lot's daughters not only dishonored their father, but they committed incest with him. All of this raises a host of questions such as: Where did they get the wine from, now that they were living in the cave? Why was Lot so foolish that he allowed himself to be plied with excessive wine? Hadn't they all just seen the dramatically powerful hand of God in judgment for the unbridled perversion in the towns that had just been destroyed? When and how did the daughters tell their father what had happened, and what was his reaction? Why did God continue such a family line, given the sin of those involved?

Both women, however, did become pregnant by their father. The older woman had a son, whom she named Moab, likely meaning "of the father," or "from father," who became the ancestor of the Moabite nation (v. 37). The younger woman also had a son, whom she named Ben-Ammi, meaning "son of a relative" or "son of my people," who likewise became an ancestor of the nation of Ammonites (v. 38).

Even though the Moabites and Ammonites are called the "sons/descendants of Lot" (Deuteronomy 2:9, 19), they are excluded from Israel's worship (Deuteronomy 23:3–4). However, this exclusion seems to rest on the fact that they did not greet the Israelites as they journeyed towards the Promised Land with bread and water, but instead hired Balaam to curse them (Numbers 22:4–20; Deuteronomy 23:4).

Conclusions

1. God sent two angels to Sodom to check on the "outcry" that had come up to heaven. They received convincing proof that the Cities of the Plain had become altogether consumed by their practice of evil, sin, and wickedness.
2. God partially answered Lot's prayer even though he could not find ten persons to justify sparing Sodom and Gomorrah, Yet the Lord allowed one city, Zoar, to be spared so Lot could go there instead of going to the mountains.
3. Lot's wife looked back and so she perished on the way to Zoar. Why she looked back is not known. Did she long for all her abandoned possessions?
4. Lot's two daughters paid a big price for not separating themselves from the world and its culture.

Questions for Thought or Discussion

1. After we are shown the episode of the deep sexual distraction of the men of Sodom at the door of Lot's home, why would Lot choose to live with his family in that environment?

2. Why did Lot apparently do nothing to stop the marriage of his two daughters to such sexual perverts as this city seemed to breed? What kind of future trouble did he think these men might evidence had the marriage gone through?

3. Suggest some reasons why Lot's wife looked back after being warned not to do so.

4. Was God bringing grace and mercy to bear on the sin of the two daughters by permitting them to become pregnant?

Lesson 9

Abraham and Abimelech, King of Gerar

Genesis 20:1–18; 21:1–34

"Yes, I know you [Abimelech] did this with a clear conscience, and so I [the Lord] have kept you from sinning against me." – Genesis 20:6b

These two chapters in Genesis, 20 and 21, focus on Abraham's relationship with other nations. The text begins with the announcement that Abraham, after staying at Hebron at the Oaks of Mamre for some twenty years (Genesis 13, 18), broke camp and moved farther south and west in the Negev desert to sojourn in the town of Gerar (20:1). Gerar was located about halfway between Gaza and Beersheba. In fact, in chapter 21 it is noted that Abraham was still sojourning in Gerar, which means the events of these two chapters take place in the "land of the Philistines" (21:23b, 34).

In the earlier chapters of Genesis, we had read about such Amorites as Mamre, Eshcol, and Aner, who lived near Hebron and who were allies with Abraham. But it is clear from Genesis 23 that over the last two decades the Hittites had moved into the area—a fact that seems to be substantiated by recent archaeological discoveries. If this population shift from an Amorite base to a Hittite plurality was really happening, then it makes Abraham's move from Hebron more understandable, for he would have searched for a place that was more secure for his family to live than at Hebron.

Abraham moved to a place "between Kadesh and Shur" (20:1). Kadesh was also called Kadesh Barnea, a town on the southern border of Canaan, at the very edge of the Negev, while Shur would have been close to the borders of Egypt. Somewhere between these two sites was located the town of Gerar.

Abraham and Sarah's Secret – 20:1–18

It now had been thirty years since Abraham and Sarah had resorted to using the lie they had made (20:13), claiming Sarah was Abraham's "sister." This was done ostensibly to preserve Abraham's life, for when Pharaoh saw how beautiful Sarah was, he wanted her for his harem (Genesis 12:10–20). She must have been a beauty. Interestingly, one of the

Dead Sea Scrolls said her beauty rested in her fingernails, which is the best we can do in "nailing" this claim down!

In Gerar, Abraham once again pulled the same stunt he had used on Pharaoh, claiming "she is my sister" (20:2)—a lie, of course. So "Abimelech, the king of Gerar, sent for Sarah and took her" (v. 2b). ("Abimelech" means "my father is king" in Hebrew and may be a royal title, as is "Pharaoh.") F. B. Meyer summed it up this way:

> During that time, he [Abraham] had been growing and learning much. But alas! the snake was scotched, not killed. The weeds were cut down, not eradicated. The dry-rot had been checked; but the rotten timbers had not been cut away. Never boast yourself [men and women in Christ] against once-cherished sins; only by God's grace are they kept in check; and if you cease to abide in Christ, they will revive and revisit you . . .[1]

Sarah was taken into Abimelech's household, but what in Genesis 12:10–20 was developed into a full narrative is here condensed into a single verse as the sin is repeated for a second time in the life of the patriarch! But instead of going on to focus the story on Sarah, the text instead concentrates its attention on Abimelech, the king of the Philistines at Gerar.

However, God appeared to Abimelech in a dream one night (20:3). God's words to the king were ominous: "You are as good as dead because of the woman you have taken; she is a married woman." The Bible writer is intending to show how innocent this Philistine king was, for even before he pleads his own innocence, the writer wants to make sure we do not judge otherwise (v. 4). No wonder, then, that the king immediately proclaimed his innocence:

> "Lord, will you destroy an innocent nation? Did he not say to me, 'She is my sister,' and didn't she also say, 'He is my brother'? I have done this with a clear conscience and clean hands." (4b–5)

Abraham tried to justify himself (v. 11) by claiming that what he said was actually a half-truth. Sarah was, it is true, his sister in the same sense that Lot was his brother. She was Abraham's niece, the daughter of Haran, his brother on his father's side. Abraham's father, Terah, must have had two wives, one by whom he had Haran and another by whom he had Sarah. Nevertheless, the claim was a pretentious lie. This raises the question of whether we believers are always bound to tell the whole truth. F. B. Meyer clarifies the answer:

> We are not bound to tell the whole truth [just] to gratify an idle curiosity; but we are bound not to withhold the one item, which another should know before completing a bargain, if the knowledge of it should materially alter the result. A lie consists in the motive quite as much as in the actual words. On the other hand, like Abraham, we may utter true words, meaning them to convey a false impression, and in the sight of Heaven we are guilty of a deliberate and shameful falsehood.[2]

But what about King Abimelech's claim to have a "clear conscience" (v. 5b)? The word "conscience" is derived from the Latin *conscientia*, which, like the Greek *suneidesis*, means "co-knowledge." "It denotes an inner witness to moral responsibility, the inherent human capacity to distinguish between good and evil."[3] The Old Testament, without using the word in most translations, shows this experience in "David's heart smote him" (1 Samuel 24:5; 2 Samuel 24:10). But it is the New Testament that teaches:

> Man has in the depths of his personality a moral monitor which sin has affected, but not destroyed, placing him in touch with the objective moral order of the universe. That order is translated into human awareness by means of the conscience. That it does not arise from cultural mores can be seen when men press for moral reforms that directly challenge social patterns. . . . A good conscience is the basis for accepting transcendent law, and a bad conscience [is the result of] the self-judgment which God will complement in the future in his own judgment. (Romans 2:16)[4]

Nevertheless, Abraham's conduct was cowardly. He put at risk Sarah's virtue and even the divine plan of a coming promised seed. What was he thinking in doing this? He seemed to have risked an awful lot! Surely his was a license of presumption and a decision to allow his wife to pass through this ordeal while he stood to one side seemingly uninvolved! Where was his faith now? He valued his own safety and existence over the promises of God! Could the Philistines have touched even the hair on his head if God had not permitted it? Hadn't he learned his lesson from the last time he did this, in Egypt?

The Almighty God has access to all that goes on in the minds of mortals, saved and unsaved, as well as with the facts of the situation. Again, God came to Abimelech in a dream and told him he was as good as a dead man (v. 3b). This threat, of course, was with the implied condition that Abimelech would touch Sarah and take her as his own wife. Given such a stern admonition, it is clear that God regards adultery as a most-heinous crime. Even though this warning is addressed to a single individual, all of us who read God's word here should hear how assuredly God judges this grievous sin whenever it is practiced; God surely hates adultery! The reason for such a stern warning was because Sarah was indeed another man's wife (v. 3d). Abimelech could not take her without infringing on another man's rights or on the solemn covenant that existed between Abraham, Sarah and God (Proverbs 2:17; Malachi 2:14). Marriage is a three-way covenant between not just a couple but also with God!

Interestingly enough, judgment would have come on the whole "nation" had their leader sinned against Sarah and Abraham (v. 4b). These words, about destroying a nation, seem to reference the recent downfall of Sodom and Gomorrah, all of which had left an impact on the countryside surrounding the cities of the Plain. Abimelech seems to be saying, "I am aware that you have slain these nations for their notorious participation in sin and the evil debauchery they have committed, but Lord, we are not such a nation."

God acknowledged Abimelech's plea of ignorance about Sarah's marriage to Abraham was correct. However, even though Abimelech was acquitted of the whole charge in this matter, there still remained some marks of divine displeasure. Verses 17 and 18 teach that God's omniscient eye could still see mixtures of evil in that conduct, for that is why God "kept [Abimelech] from sinning against me" (v. 6b). Here is striking proof of God's mercy and condescension to us in our mortal states! God's honest intention was that Abimelech should not violate the sanctity of the marriage covenant. Therefore, God ordered that this Philistine king should not touch Sarah, for this couple had been chosen to carry out his Promise-Plan for all humanity. Moreover, "Abraham is a prophet, and he will pray for you and you will live" (v. 7).

Early the next morning, Abimelech arose and summoned his officials to come at that early hour for a critical cabinet meeting (v. 8). When he told them of his dream, they were frightened (v. 8b). It's easy to see why! Abimelech called Abraham and went into a well-grounded rebuke for what he had perpetrated on this king and his people (v. 9). What a surprising change of roles, for now the heathen Abimelech became the prophet of the Lord to rebuke his prophet! Even so, considering what Abraham had done to him, his rebuke was fairly mild (vv. 9–10). Only once did Abimelech slip into some gentle sarcasm as he addressed Sarah with these words: "I am giving your *'brother'* a thousand shekels of silver" (v. 16).

Abimelech also gave to Abraham sheep, oxen, male and female servants as he restored Sarah to the patriarch (v. 14). He also generously offered him free range to go and live wherever he liked in his territory (v. 15).

Hagar and Ishmael Cast Out – 21:1–34

The Son Isaac Is Born to Abraham and Sarah – 21:1–7

God promised in 18:10, "I will surely return to you about this time next year and Sarah your wife will have a son." After focusing on the Philistines for the last three chapters, the writer now returns to the promise about a son! Moreover, three times the text emphasizes that the birth happened "as he said" or "had promised"—meaning, of course, as God had said (21:1–2). The significance of the announcement of Isaac's birth is underscored by the use of the verb "visited/was gracious" (Hebrew *paqad*, "to visit"). This note showed that when God "visited" in the Old Testament, it was in a twofold way—he showed his mercy in fulfilling his promise, and he also inflicted judgment or carried out threats against the wicked. In this case, it showed his mercy!

Abraham bore this son in old age—in his one hundredth year of living (vv. 2, 5), but that son Isaac came at precisely the time God had promised! Some very-similar language is used in Joshua 21:43–45, which points out that the Lord gave the Israelites the possessions of the land according to all that he had sworn unto their fathers! Not one good thing that God had promised had failed to happen; it all came to pass! But we must not miss the miracle here in Genesis 21 either, for both parents were by now quite old. Even though the promise had been given long ago (Genesis 18), the text reiterates the fact that "the LORD did for Sarah what he had promised" (v. 1b); God does not want us to miss this point. So when Isaac was eight days old, Abraham circumcised him as God had commanded (v. 4). Nothing is of greater importance in the eyes of God than our implicit obedience to all that he has commanded us. This is especially true in the matter of sacramental institutions such as circumcision. This does not mean we should fabricate new observances and enforce them by promises or threats, as some do.

God had given to Sarah an occasion to "laugh" (v. 6). Everyone who hears about Isaac's birth, she said, would join with her in expressing their joy and "laughter." Anyway, Sarah went on marveling as she exclaimed, "Who would have said to Abraham that Sarah would have children? Yet I indeed have borne him a son in his old age" (v. 7).

The child Isaac grew, and Abraham threw a great feast on the day Isaac was weaned (v. 8b). In the ancient Near East, this would have been when Isaac was about three years old; recall that when Samuel was weaned, he was old enough to be left with the priest Eli for serving in the Tabernacle (1 Samuel 3; 2 Chronicles 26:16).

Hagar and Ishmael Are Cast Out of Abraham's Tent – 21:9–21

This part of Genesis 21 is very much like the events recorded in Genesis 16 and 17. But Sarah noticed something that troubled her. She saw Hagar's son Ishmael "mocking" (Hebrew *metzahek*) Isaac. The Hebrew word is derived from the same root as the word behind Isaac's name. This must have been a type of malicious teasing calculated to irritate and vex Isaac, if not to sneer at God's promise in his life (21:9). That is how the Apostle Paul understood this mocking as well, for he said Ishmael "persecuted Isaac" (Galatians 4:29). This mocking, the text also emphasized, was done by the son of Hagar, "the Egyptian." The Hebrew word definitely means "to mock," for it is the same word used to describe how Lot's potential sons-in-law reacted when they were told of the coming destruction of Sodom (19:4). It is also the word used by Potiphar's wife when she falsely accused Joseph of "making sport" of her (Genesis 39:14, 17). The Israelites used the same word when they worshiped the golden calf and rose up in "revelry" (Exodus 32:6). Only in the case of Isaac, where he "caressed" his wife (26:8), does the word have a favorable connotation; otherwise it carries an evil and negative sense.

Whether Hagar approved of Ishmael's mocking behavior is unclear, but Sarah immediately ordered Abraham, after this incident, to "get rid of" [literally, "to drive out"] that slave woman, for that slave woman's son will never share in the inheritance with my son Isaac" (v. 10). Sarah wanted some kind of action taken by her husband that would ensure this boy would never be in line to receive the inheritance that should go to her son.

Early the next morning, Abraham, as custom demanded, provided Hagar with bread and water, placing them on her shoulder, and sent them on their way (21:14). Hagar then wandered about in the wilderness of Beersheba. Hagar did not go to Egypt immediately, as we might have assumed, but she went north from the town of Gerar where Abraham had been living (v. 14b).

Later, the water Abraham had given her ran out, and Ishmael began to faint and cry out in discomfort. In an effort to make him somewhat comfortable, Hagar placed him in the shade of a desert bush, and she retired to a spot nearby that was within "bow-shot" of the boy (vv. 15–16). She could not bear to watch her son die, and with that she too began to cry (v. 16b).

But as the boy continued to cry (v. 17a), suddenly "the angel of God" called to Hagar from heaven: "What is the matter, Hagar? Do not be afraid; God has heard the boy crying, as he lies there. Lift the boy up and take him by the hand, for I will make him into a great nation" (vv. 17–18). The promise of making Ishmael a nation known for its greatness is a repeat of the promise made in 16:10 and 17:20. This angel of the Lord must be the same Christophany we saw in 16:7. God opened Hagar's eyes, and she saw a well of water nearby (v. 19). So she went and gave Ishmael a drink. God continued to be with this boy as he grew up and as he lived in the Desert of Paran. As God promised, he did become a great nation, and his mother did get for him a wife from Egypt (vv. 20–21).

Abraham and Abimelech Make an Alliance – 21:22–34

Abimelech, the king of Gerar—who we haven't heard from while all this was going on—came with Phicol, the commander of his armies, to visit Abraham (v. 22). The pagan king began with a wonderful testimony about Abraham: "God is with you in everything you do" (v. 22b). In light of that affirmation, Abimelech wanted to form an alliance with Abraham, thereby treating him as an equal partner and not a nomadic visitor. Moreover, if God was blessing Abraham, then it might just prove beneficial to be allied with him if possible. He reminded Abraham that he had treated him with kindness even though Abraham had been living in that country as an alien (v. 23). Thus the king asked him to swear an oath that he would not deal falsely with him or his descendants in the future.

Abraham agreed, but he had one complaint. His servants had dug a well of water in the desert, but Abimelech's servants had seized it as their own (v. 25). Abraham wanted this matter straightened out before formalizing the alliance. Abimelech replied that this was the first he had heard about the seizure (v. 26). It seems Abimelech quickly assured Abraham that the well would be returned immediately, though, and with this minor matter taken care of, the two men proceeded to formally seal their alliance. Abraham brought "seven ewe lambs from his flock" (v. 28), and Abimelech asked what the meaning of this was. The answer is in the fact that the word used for "treaty" in v. 27 is the same Hebrew word for "to cut" or "to make a covenant" (Hebrew *karat*; see 15:18). This ceremony took place in

Abraham's territory, so he provided the animals required to seal the alliance. The animals were like earnest money that secured the change of ownership of the property. It was for this reason that that site became known as "Beersheba," meaning "well of oath" (v. 31). Once the alliance was made, Abimelech and Phicol returned to the land of the Philistines (v. 32).

Interestingly enough, Abraham planted a tamarisk tree as a memorial of where "he [had] called upon the name of the LORD, the Eternal God" (v. 33). Abraham ended up staying in that land for a long time (v. 34).

Conclusions

1. Telling half-truths is still considered lying in God's judgment, especially when the one to whom only a portion of the truth is told had a right to know all the facts in order to make a correct or wise decision.
2. Taking another man's wife is so serious a matter that God pronounces the one who has done such a dead man. That behooves us to be most careful in the way we respond to other household's spouses.
3. The promises God made with Abraham in Genesis 12:2–3 and 15:2–6 are unconditional and eternal in the effect.
4. God promised Ishmael that he would become a great nation as well. This is the basis for the large increase in the Arab and Islamic nations.
5. Abraham made an alliance with the king of Gerar by "cutting" the animals and forming an aisle as in Genesis 15.

Questions for Thought or Discussion

1. What would have happened to our salvation and God's Promise-Plan if Abraham had refused to drive away Hagar and Ishmael? What troubled Abraham in doing this?
2. What would have happened to God's Promise-Plan if King Abimelech would have had sexual relations with Sarah? What would have happened in that case to Abimelech?
3. What role does our conscience play in making a moral decision?
4. How was Abimelech able to see that God had blessed Abraham in everything he did?

Lesson 10

The Testing of Abraham
and the Binding of Isaac

Genesis 22:1–24

"Take your son, your only son . . . [and] sacrifice him." – Genesis 22:2

Genesis 22 is both the best-known event in the life of Abraham, yet it is also one of the most baffling narratives from the standpoint of the request God makes of the patriarch. To put this episode in context, Abraham has just sent off one child, Ishmael, but now it appears as if he is about to lose his second son, Isaac. So what's going on in this narrative?

The Testing of Abraham – Genesis 22:1–2

The narrative begins by stating that it was "some time later" that God "tested Abraham," so Isaac was growing up (22:1). The Hebrew term here for "testing," *nisah*, means "to test, to try, to prove." But some translations instead say God "tempted" Abraham, and this demands an immediate correction. As James 1:13 makes abundantly clear, "God cannot be tempted by evil, nor does he tempt anyone." God may, however, allow his servants to experience special testing—not to give him information, but to manifest to themselves and others the tendencies and directions of their hearts.

This Hebrew term "to test" can be used in several ways: (1) as illustrated by the Queen of Sheba in 1 Kings 10:1, she came to King Solomon's court to see for herself how great was his wisdom by plying him with questions. (2) This term is also used of God's dealings with people to see how consistent their walk with the Lord was (Exodus 16:4; Deuteronomy 8:2, 16; 13:3; 2 Chronicles 32:31). (3) This term is also used of mortals who presume to test God to determine how adequate God's power is (Exodus 17:2, 7; Numbers 14:22; Psalm 26:2; Isaiah 7:12).

The one who tempts humanity is Satan (1 Corinthians 7:5). We can also be tempted by our own desires and lusts (James 1:14). Thus, we must observe two key differences between tempting and testing: It is Satan who tempts us, but it is God who tests us. Satan tempts us to destroy us (1 Peter

5:8; James 1:15; Romans 6:23), but God tests us to strengthen us (Exodus 20:20; Deuteronomy 8:2). Moreover, God tests us so that "in the end it might go well with [us]" (Deuteronomy 8:16).

Granted, the test God gave Abraham was a staggering challenge, for it asked him to surrender the son on whom God's whole Promise-Plan rested. Moreover, this divine test came suddenly and abruptly, as if out of nowhere. Added to that was the fact that the test gave very succinct commands, using just three simple imperatives: "take," "go," and "sacrifice [Isaac]" (22:2). God did not give an explanation for his command. He gave the order: Abraham was to "take your only son [Isaac], whom you love," and sacrifice him. Isaac was the *only* son" as distinct from Ishmael, who had been expelled. It was in this sense, then, that Abraham would have understood it.

A twin pair of covenant promises had dominated the gifts God would give to Abraham up to this point. However, with the commands to "take," "go," and "sacrifice" Isaac, Abraham's *only* son," an enormous obstacle arises that seems to test God's "friend" to the breaking point. Note that the previous chapter had ended with "Abraham call[ing] on the name of the Eternal God" (21:33). God had revealed himself as "El Shaddai, God Almighty" (17:1), but what Abraham had not seen as yet was the Eternal God who was unchangeable and independent of change in time or circumstances. However, the call to sacrifice his son—this was brand-new and totally unexpected to Abraham! But he knew the voice of God all too certainly, so without protest or murmur (though perhaps with a thousand questions crowding into his mind and soul), he immediately prepared to go the next morning to do as God had commanded.

Of course Abraham knew that one of the first principles of Canaanite religion was that pagan parents should give their firstborn as a human sacrifice for their transgressions, the fruit of their bodies for the sins of their souls. Such human sacrifice, however, though only later explicitly forbidden in Scripture, was surely understood by Abraham as utterly inconsistent with the God he knew as "friend." On the altars of Moab, Phoenicia, Carthage, and later even in sinful Israel, godless families practiced this monstrous sacrifice. But this type of human sacrifice to Molech was not what Abraham understood God to be asking of him. What these cultures did share, though, was the need for a substitute.

The Binding of Isaac – 22:3–14

The writer slows down the narrative by giving us a host of deliberate details of the patriarch's preparation for the journey to Mount Moriah (v. 3). If God had appeared to Abraham in a dream the night previously, then certainly he was up "Early the next morning" and busy carrying out preparations to obey the commands God had given to him (v. 3a). Abraham himself promptly saddled his donkey (v. 3a), split enough wood for the sacrifice (v. 3c), and got ready for his journey north with his son Isaac and two of his servants (v. 3b). Apparently, he said nothing to his wife Sarah, nor did he confide what God had asked of him to anyone else, despite what must have been a ton of questions which plagued his heart and mind. In fact, this old man, with his son Isaac and two servants was already on his way when the herdsmen were just beginning to stir from their sleep that night, or when the long lines of cattle would be led off to their numerous grazing grounds. The call of God did not produce in Abraham any kind of outrage from any instincts of protecting the life of his son. He would avoid discussing the matter with any of his fellowmen or even with his wife Sarah; instead, he must be off to obey the instruction from God.

What must have those three days of quiet meditation and rumination been like (for no conversation is recorded during these days of walking from Beersheba to Moriah, a distance of something close to fifty miles). Walking across the hot earth must have been horrible for this man with a heavy heart. But it is in such a process as this, time is given for mortals to wait upon God in these protracted periods of silence. In spite of the sorrow of his soul, it was necessary for Abraham to keep it to himself lest his son or his servants might guess the agony his soul was under. So, on he walked in silence!

Finally, on the third day he saw the place—Mount Moriah—that had been divinely appointed for him to carry out God's commands (vv. 2, 4). Mount Moriah is identified with the same mountain in Jerusalem on which the Temple of Solomon was built (2 Chronicles 3:1). This was where the threshing floor of Araunah, the Jebusite, was located. The name Araunah or Ornan is probably a Hurrian name; he was the one from whom King David bought the land, on which he later purposed to build the temple for the Lord (2 Samuel 24:18–25; 1 Chronicles 21:28–30). The name "Moriah" may mean "my teacher + Yah," *mori* + Yah[weh]." Others connect it with the verb *ra'a*, "to see," thus meaning "seen by Yah[weh]" or "vision of Yah[weh]."

The severity of the test for Abraham can be seen in the intensity of the three descriptions given of Isaac: his "only" son, his "precious" son, the son "whom he loves" (22:2)!

Verse 2 raises the key ethical question about whether God really asked Abraham to sacrifice his son Isaac. In Western culture, the classic expression of this dilemma is in Søren Kierkegaard's 1843 book *Fear and Trembling*.[1] As Kierkegaard tells the story, there are two Abrahams: one "the ethical Abraham" who sees the moral law as universal, and the other Abraham is "the knight of faith," who knows of a higher law than a universal moral law, which permits him to take the life of another because it is a "teleological suspension of the ethical." In other words, for Kierkegaard, Abraham was torn between his desire to obey God and his question as to whether this really was a command from God.

But the cult of child sacrifice seen in the pagan worship of Molech was later repudiated explicitly in Leviticus 18:21: "You shall not give any of your children to devote them by fire to Molech." This was a sacrifice not ever approved by God.

On the third day, Abraham spotted the place called Mount Moriah. Abraham addressed the two young servants (Hebrew *ne`arim*), who were trekking along with them, "Stay here with the donkey; the lad and I, we will worship [on this mountain], and we will return again" (v. 5). Some think that Abraham's words were meant to hide from his servants what he was up to on the mountain, but Hebrews 11:17–19 takes these words to be a powerful statement that God is able to raise his son Isaac up from the dead!

The wood for the sacrifice Abraham piled on Isaac's shoulders, but he took the more dangerous things such as the fire and the knife as the two of them began to climb the mountain (v. 6). It was at this point Isaac became aware of the fact that something important was missing, so he asked, "Father? The fire and the wood are here, but where is the lamb for the burnt offering?" (v. 7) Abraham answered, "God himself will provide the lamb for the burnt offering, my son" (v. 8). "And the two of them went on together" (v. 8b). Isaac makes no attempt to raise any more questions, but he must have thought: *Where does Father think he can get a lamb on this mountain? Lambs don't grow on trees. And what is the purpose of the ropes, I wonder?*

But by now they had come to the place on Moriah where Abraham was told to go. First, Abraham built an altar, as he had done in Genesis 12:7, 8; 13:18, and where, on the heels of completing the construction of the altar,

God had also previously given to him a divine promise. But this time, Abraham, after he had laid the wood on the altar, began to "bind" (Hebrew `aqad, "to bind," which is used only here in the Bible) his son. This passage became the famous passage called the "Aqedah of Isaac" in Jewish theology. Then his father laid Isaac on the altar on top of the pile of wood (v. 9). Surprisingly, Isaac made no attempt to impede the actions of his father. He certainly had grown physically able and strong enough by this time to have put up quite a fight against his father's actions if he had wanted to do so, but no such skirmish took place between father and son.

The word verse 10 uses is the sacrificial word to "slay," or to "slaughter" (Hebrew *shahat*). The instrument Abraham planned to incorporate into this sacrifice was a "knife" (v. 10). The blade had already been raised high, perhaps flashing in the rays of the bright noonday sun. The moment for obedience had come. Things were beginning to look extremely grim, for death was near at hand for Abraham's "only" son.

Suddenly, God's messenger called from heaven; "the Angel of the LORD" halted the onslaught and the unfolding drama by urgently repeating, "Abraham, Abraham." To this summons the father responded: "Here am I" (v. 11). Then followed the wonderful words of release and deliverance:

> Do not lay a hand on the boy. Do not do anything to him. Now I know that you fear God, because you have not withheld from me your son, your only son. (12)

Abraham was willing to give his best and his costliest to God, after allowing his gifts to pass through the fire of surrendering to God's will. Thus God gave back to Abraham refined gold. No wonder, then, that Abraham called that place "the LORD sees/will provide" (*Yahweh Yir'eh*). There is a wordplay on the name Moriah, for it captures the Hebrew verb "to see" (*ra'a*) and the Hebrew verb "he will provide" (*yir'eh*).

It may be asked, however, that when God said, "Now I know that you fear God," did God not already know what Abraham's attitude was? Of course the Lord knew Abraham's thoughts, but the expression "now I know" must be viewed as a human way of speaking about the fact that now Abraham clearly showed his complete faith in God.

As Abraham no doubt was recovering from the drama of what he had just experienced, he looked up and "there in a thicket he saw a ram, caught by his horns" (v. 13). How appropriate! How timely! How instructive, for

Abraham "went over and took the ram and sacrificed it as a burnt offering instead of his son" (v. 13b). Here, suddenly, was God's substitute, his provision in place of his son. This more than anything else illustrates the biblical doctrine of substitution. Abraham's act helps us to understand the sacrifice God made for us in providing us his salvation, for Yeshua went to the cross in order to save us from the guilt and defects of our sin. What is more, Isaac's gentle submission in the hands of his father, as he was laid upon the altar and perhaps as Abraham placed the knife at the throat of his son Isaac—all of this gives us a better insight into Yeshua's obedience and his substitution for our sin.

The angel of the Lord came a second time to Abraham from heaven (v. 15) and this is what he promised:

> I swear by myself, declares the LORD, that because you have done this and have not withheld your son, your only son, I will surely bless you and make your descendants as numerous as the stars in the sky and as the sand on the seashore. Your descendants will take possession of the cities of their enemies, and through your offspring all nations on earth will be blessed, because you have obeyed me (16–18).

In this manner God provided a surrogate for Isaac, "another ram" (Hebrew `ayil `ahar, "another ram")! We should not miss the irony of this well-authenticated reading of "another ram." Many commentators wish to emend this reading to say, "one ram," but the text put it this way: Isaac was for all practical purposes the first ram, but now to the surprise of both Abraham and Isaac, "Lo and behold, here was another ram!" (v. 13)

Even though Abraham had answered Isaac's inquiry "Where is the lamb/sheep?" by promising God would provide the "sheep," it turned out to be a "ram." There is no explanation as to why the Lord sent a different animal from the one Abraham assumed God would provide (v. 8). This patriarch had offered a ram earlier (15:9). However, "rams" occur in two prominent places in the Old Testament: at the ordination of priests (Leviticus 8–9; especially 9:2–4) and on the Day of Atonement (Leviticus 16:1, 3). Thus the ram is associated with the priesthood and the atonement. So the place is named by Abraham "Yahweh Yireh," meaning "God sees/provides" (v. 14).

Abraham returned with his servants back to Beersheba, where he had started out from in Genesis 21:33. (v. 19). Why nothing is said about Isaac returning with him and his two servants is left unsaid.

The Relatives of Abraham – 22:20–24

Attention is focused once more on the homeland from which Abraham and Lot had come. By doing so, we are given background material as a source for the future bride for Isaac in Genesis 24, named Rebekah (v. 23). Isaac will marry into the Nahor family, Abraham's brother. Nahor has twelve sons, eight by his wife Milcah and four by his concubine Reumah. The twelve Aramean tribes are named after these sons.

Both Abraham's marriage to his half-sister and Nahor's marriage to his niece (Genesis 11:29) are outlawed by later Levitical law (Leviticus 18:9, 11; 20:17; 20:20). But it appears that in the Patriarchal times, such marriages were allowed. Moreover, both Abraham and Nahor had children by a wife and by a concubine.

Conclusions

1. Abraham "binds" Isaac as an offering to the Lord, but the Lord provides a substitute instead of receiving Isaac as that offering. Thus, in this story the person to be sacrificed is spared, but the Lord on the cross was not excused the suffering, but he himself suffered.
2. The Lord ordered Abraham with his command to take his son and go sacrifice him on Mount Moriah. How did this "test" Abraham?
3. Abraham raised his eyes to see caught in the thicket a ram, which became "another ram" for sacrifice.
4. Mount Moriah means "my teacher is God." But it may also mean "God sees/provides."

Questions for Thought or Discussion

1. How is the word "fear" used in 22:12, "Now I know you fear me"?
2. How is Mark 10:45 connected to the theology of Genesis 22?
3. What makes Mount Moriah so special, not only in the past, but also in the future?
4. Do you think that the split wood placed on the altar in Genesis 22 is in anyway a type or symbol of the cross of Messiah?
5. Why was the substituted animal switched from a sheep/lamb to a ram?

Lesson 11

Sarah's Death and the Purchase of the Cave of Machpelah

Genesis 23:1–20

"Sarah lived to be a hundred and twenty-seven years old." – Genesis 23:1

The Life and Death of Sarah – 23:1–2b

It seems remarkable that Sarah is the only female mentioned in Scripture whose age, death, and burial are distinctly noted. Whereas she had already reached 65 years of age when Abraham departed from Haran with Lot and had lived with Abraham as a fellow pilgrim for 62 years in Canaan, she passed on to glory at 127 years of age, preceding her husband in death by 38 years (23:1). In fact, Sarah served as a model of conjugal fidelity and love for believing "daughters" who would follow her, as 1 Peter 2:6 comments:

> Like Sarah, who obeyed Abraham and called him lord. You are her daughters if you do what is right and do not give way to fear.

This praise of her is offered even though there are very few events in the Bible where she is the center of the action. Yet she still is worthy of praise by the generations that follow her. She lived her life in a noiseless way, yet the fact that there were few negative remarks made about her speaks well of her devotedness to God and the way she went about her domestic duties. Her life and walk with the Lord were therefore unobtrusive and amiable.

Sarah died in the town of Kiriath Arba, which was later known as Hebron (v. 2). Abraham, after he had enjoyed perhaps the tenderest of all relationships with Sarah for as many years as many in our day live (a total of some 62 years) is now called upon to feel the pangs of separation. Abraham must have been away from her at the time of her death, perhaps shepherding the flock in some verdant pasture in the Negev, so he had to "come" back to Hebron (v. 2).

Hebron originally was known as Kiriath Arba (literally, "the town of Arba"), situated some 27 miles south of Jerusalem, east of a chain of hills that intersects the county from north to south. It stands on the slope of an eminence, whose summit has some ruins on it. In those days, Arba was a prominent member of one of the Amorite tribes living near Hebron. Hebron was also known by the name of nearby Mamre (Genesis 13:18; 23:19; 35:27), the name of another of Abraham's allies and Amorite friends (14:13, 24). As a matter of fact, the name Kiriath Arba could also be rendered "the town/city of four." This was to acknowledge the possible sites of Mamre, Aner, Eschol, and Hebron, or perhaps as the rabbis loved to analyze it, the towns celebrating four illustrious men: Adam, Abraham, Isaac, and Jacob! But Adam and Eve were not buried in Hebron, so these four names will not work for the name Arba!

For more information about Hebron, we turn to Joshua 14:13–15:

> Then Joshua blessed Caleb son of Jephunneh and gave him Hebron as his inheritance. So, Hebron has belonged to Caleb son of Jephunneh the Kenizzite ever since, because he followed the LORD, the God of Israel, wholeheartedly. (Hebron used to be called Kiriath Arba after Arba, who was the greatest man among the Anakites [giants].)

Whatever the real origin of Hebron was, Numbers 13:22 seems to say that it certainly must have been one of the most ancient of cities, for it was built seven years before Zoan/Tanis in Egypt was built, the capital of the region of Lower Egypt. Moreover, when the Israelites first came to Hebron, it was possessed by the Anakim before Caleb took possession of it. Later Hebron must have been taken over by the Hittites, and then it was later assigned to the Levites and labelled a city of refuge. Later still, David set up his court in Hebron for the first seven years of his reign in Judah. Then during the Babylonian exile, the Edomites captured Hebron and gave it the name of Idumea, which it continued to be called long after the Edomites had left Hebron as the capital of their district. Hebron is now merely a village that is known by the name of "El Khalil," meaning "the friend," because it was the residence of Abraham, who was called "the friend of God." The town of Hebron may even appear in the New Testament in the personage of Judas Iscariot, rendered by some as "Judas, man of Kiriath."

Abraham's Mourning and Bargaining for the Sepulcher – 23:2c–16

Abraham returned home to mourn for his wife Sarah (v. 2c). This event happened some 36 or 37 years after the birth of Isaac (17:1, 21:5). The fact that Abraham mourned for Sarah was altogether proper and suitable, for his loss was great, so it was most natural that he would give vent to his feelings. Believers are to mourn and weep with those who mourn and express their grief and sadness (Romans 12:14). In fact, the person who does not weep on such an occasion is not thereby to be judged more the man for having held back his tears in a so-called "manly way." Even Yeshua wept at the gravesite of Lazarus for his deceased friend. There is nothing abhorrent or lacking in manly virtue if a believer mourns in the face of his own loss or that of his friend's loss. We all must learn to let the tears flow when the grief and the pain well-up within us, either for ourselves or for others.

But just as there is a time for weeping, so there is a time to refrain from grief and to get on with the cares of life (v. 3). Therefore, Abraham went to the sons of Heth, the grand children of Ham, known as the Hittites, and began to make arrangements for the purchase of Sarah's sepulcher.

Abraham began his request this way in verse 4:

> I am a foreigner and stranger among you. Sell me some property for a burial site so I can bury my dead.

Thus, the man, who had been promised some one hundred years ago by the Lord that one day he would own the whole country, was as yet without even enough of the land to bury a place for his deceased wife! It would become evident in subsequent days that this burial site would first of all be for Sarah, later it would be for Abraham himself, and then later still it would be for Isaac and Rebekah as well as for Jacob and Leah. Today these graves are situated deep beneath the upper level of the Mosque of Abraham, a Muslim shrine in Hebron.

So now, toward the close of a long and labor-filled life, we see Abraham finally obtaining his first inheritance. For now close to a century, Abraham confesses to the sons of Heth that he had been merely a "stranger and sojourner" in the land. Hebrews 11:13 makes the same point, that they had "confessed that they were strangers and pilgrims on earth." But this assessment of the situation was not new, for Israel was taught the same point of view when they were about to enter the land in Leviticus 25:23, "The land shall not be sold forever; for the land is mine, for you are strangers and sojourners with me." No one less than even King David made the same affirmation, "For I am a stranger with you and a sojourner, as all my fathers were" (Psalm 39:11). Surely, all mortals have sensed somewhat of the same vagabond spirit when we likewise stand by the grave of someone we love. Perhaps all of us should carry such a spirit of a pilgrim, so that when trials and disappointments come, we regard them as a typical stranger would, placing our greater hope in the eternal peace that awaits us on the other side of this life!

The Hittites responded to Abraham in an equal type of graciousness, for they acknowledge him as a "mighty prince [or, "prince of God" in their] midst" (v. 5). Surely, they had observed firsthand the favor and blessing that God had bestowed on Abraham. As a result, they assured him of their fullest cooperation and apparently offered him the choice of their burial plots (v. 6).

Abraham stood up and bowed down before the sons of Heth, the Hittites (v. 7), in a reverential act as he began to make his request. He began, "If it be well with your soul," meaning that if it was something pleasant and agreeable with their wills, hearts, and minds, would they please hear what he had to say, and would they please entreat Ephron, the son of Zohar, that he may "sell" to me the cave of Machpelah (vv. 8–9). The name "Machpelah" perhaps comes from the Hebrew *kapal*, meaning "to be double," since the cave likely consisted of two separate chambers or had two separate entrances. However, the name may just as well have come from a proper name of its owner at one time, but there still seemed to be something distinctive about the topography of the cave that gave rise in the first place to this concept of doubling in the cave of Machpelah. Moreover, this cave was at "the end of his field" (v. 9).

The verb "to give" appears four times (vv. 4, 9, 13), which also meant "to sell" in ancient Hebrew. Therefore, in a classic account of bargaining as practiced in the Near East, the serious part of beginning the purchase of the land started. This process was brought home to me in an incident related by one of my classmates at Brandeis University in the PhD program. Jack Sasson was a new student from Lebanon, as I recall. His mother was to arrive a little latter in the school term from Lebanon, just after Jack began his doctoral studies with us in Boston area. He told the humorous story of his mother's first experience of going to one of our mega grocery stores in the States. She put her groceries on the checkout counter after shopping with more choices than she had ever seen before, and then she heard the gal ringing her up say, "That will be $56.27." She responded in typical bargaining terms of her home county in Lebanon, "I'll give you $25." After a long explanation that the price would remain fixed, she expressed her sadness that if bartering was not part of the American scene in shopping, she was unhappy. Her final assessment was this: "Surely, shopping in America cannot be any fun, for all the prices are set already!"

Ephron had been sitting in the gate area, where such legal transactions normally took place, listening to all previous exchange. So Ephron responded to Abraham in the hearing of all the Hittites,

"No, my lord. . . . Listen to me. I [will] give you the field and I give you
the cave that is in it. I [will] give it to you in the presence of my people.
Bury your dead." (11)

Abraham had not been looking for a handout, but Ephron, the seller, also
wanted to be seen as being magnanimous; indeed, the "giver." To this offer,
Abraham bowed down once again before the people of the land, and he
responded to Ephron's offer: "Listen to me, if you will, [for] I will pay the
price of the field. Accept it from me so I can bury my dead there" (v. 12). It
sounded as if a deal was finally on, but what about the price. That haggling
over the price was yet to follow.

Ephron began again, "Listen to me, my lord; the land is worth four
hundred shekels of silver,[1] but what is that between me and you? Bury your
dead." (v. 14). To this offer, Abraham agreed and so he weighed out for him
the price he had named in the hearing of the Hittites (v. 16). Ephron may
have anticipated some bargaining about the price, which would have been
customary (and more fun, according to my classmate's mother). But
apparently, no price was too great for a decent burial of his beloved Sarah.
The price, however, was no bargain, for 400 shekels would amount to more
than 100 pounds of silver. Some note that David paid one-eighth that
amount—50 shekels—for the purchase of the entire temple site (2 Samuel
24:24). But King Omri paid fifteen times as much as Abraham did for a large
hill in Samaria—two talents of silver, which is 6000 shekels (1 Kings
16:24)! Ephron, of course, thought 400 shekels of silver was a somewhat
paltry amount to pay for the burial site, for he asked sort of nonchalantly,
"What is that between you and me?" But Abraham offered no resistance to
pay the amount Ephron set, nor did he attempt to get the price lowered. Even
more suggestive is the remark from other commentators: We all wonder if
the 400 shekels of silver came from the 1000 pieces of silver Abraham
received from Abimelech for Sarah (20:16)! The text does not tell us!

From recent studies of Hittite law, it may have been that Abraham was
not interested in purchasing the whole field, just the cave of Machpelah at the
end. From recent archaeological studies, it appears that if he owned the whole
field, then certain feudal obligations, such as serving in the military of the
area, would have been part of the deal. Thus the obligation for this kind of
service would shift from the seller now to the new buyer.[2] The sellers, then,
may have wanted to be free of all service obligations, so they urged Abraham
to buy the whole field even though he did not need it. It is also interesting that

"all the trees" are mentioned as part of what was being sold, because the trees were part and parcel of Hittite real-estate transactions (v. 17).

Thus, the only piece of ground that Abraham possessed, in fulfillment of God's Promise-Plan, was a grave! (v. 19–20).

Conclusions

1. Sarah passed away at 127 years of age while Abraham and Sarah were living in Hebron.
2. Later the couple moved for some time into Philistine territory at the city of Gerar, where Abraham pulled his old trick to protect his life by saying Sarah was his "sister."
3. God spared Abimelech, though he otherwise would have been as good as dead, for he acted in good conscience, but God scolded Abraham for his half-truth, and so did Abimelech!
4. The grave site for all the three patriarchs and their wives was in Hebron and is still memorialized there.

Questions for Thought or Discussion

1. Do you think a half-truth can ever qualify as the truth?
2. What legitimate role does "conscience" play in our lives as believers?
3. What role do "dreams" play in divine revelation and to what degree can we count on that form of revelation today?
4. Did Abraham sin against God when he purchased the Cave of Machpelah even though God was going to give him all of the land of Canaan?
5. Why did God leave Sarah's womb barren for so many years when he had promised a great number of descendants? Did this not give the patriarchs a late start?
6. If Abimelech is as good as dead for taking Sarah, what does this say about the seriousness of adultery in our day from God's perspective?

Lesson 12

The Servant's Prayer
for a Bride for Isaac

Genesis 24:1–67

"Then [the servant] prayed, 'O LORD God of my master Abraham, give me success today, and show kindness to my master Abraham.'"
– Genesis 24:12

In the enormous sweep of history over the pageantry of nations and their quest for recognition, it seems, at least at first, a rather-trivial event to include a whole chapter on the search for a bride for Abraham's son Isaac. Yet we have here Genesis 24, one of the longest chapters in the Bible, set aside for the marriage of Isaac. But to conclude that we are dealing with mere trivia in God's eyes is to miss the fact that the providence of our Lord is filled with his actions in moving forward even the details in the shape of his Promise-Plan for all the peoples of the earth. What to us, in our own thinking, might seem mere happenstance in the revelation of God often adds up to one of his deepest mysteries.

The "senior servant" mentioned in 24:2 is likely Eliezer, who we met in 15:2. He is chosen to lead the delegation to search for Isaac's bride. The character of this "senior servant," if we have correctly identified him as one and the same as Eliezer, is one who is charged with a commission from his master Abraham and who faithfully carries it out in detail. Eliezer shows himself as an employee who is especially worthy of being entrusted with such a task as was assigned to him, for he does not leave undone any part of the instructions he carries out (v. 12). In fact, his conduct also reflects strong credit to Abraham, for he exhibits the influence of a pious life lived in God's presence. His example of humble and exemplary conduct led to the honoring of his former hometown in the upper-northwestern part of Mesopotamia.

Eliezer Takes an Oath – 24:2–9

Abraham had been living his life between the promise of God's blessing and the fulfillment of that promise (24:1). God had been blessing the patriarch in one area after another, but now it was time to summon his senior servant—which, as we have argued, was no doubt Eliezer—for the next step in God's Promise-Plan. Some have tried to nominate one of the two "young servants" who accompanied Abraham up to Mount Moriah (22:3), but they were called in Hebrew *ne`arim*, "young men," and this servant was known in Hebrew as *zeqan*, "old," and therefore "senior"; thus, Eliezer fits better.

Abraham instructed this servant to "put your hand under my thigh" as a prelude to his taking the oath. The significance of this act at the time is not clear, but it may be a way of signifying to Abraham that his servant would carry out his desires honestly and truthfully. It may also have been a way of alluding to the covenant sign, and thus a way of invoking the presence of God on both the master and the servant.

There are only two places in Scripture where placing one's hand on another's "thigh" is found: Genesis 24:2 and 47:29. Both men were already advanced in years—Abraham, who was "very old" and Jacob, who was on his deathbed. In both cases they involved family matters—for Abraham, it dealt with getting the right girl for his son; for Jacob it was the desire to be buried with his ancestors.[1]

Surprisingly, Abraham did not explicitly require that his servant locate a bride who believed in God, but only that she should be an Aramean and not a Canaanite. Apparently the one fact implied the other! In fact, as we later discover, Rebekah's brother Laban was actually a practicing polytheist, who panicked when someone stole "his gods." But Abraham made his messenger swear he would faithfully carry out his task "by Yahweh, the God of the heavens and earth" (v. 3)—a majestic name for the Lord, reminiscent of the name used at the memorable meeting of Abraham with Melchizedek in Genesis 14:19, 22. But the testimony of Abraham's servant is all the more outstanding when put alongside of the apparent spiritual achievements of at least some of his relatives!

The place to find the right kind of wife was the place Abraham had lived for some time after he had left Ur of the Chaldees with his father Terah (v. 4). The instructions to the servant were all good and well, but the servant asked, "What if the woman will not come, or her family will not allow her to leave their home?" (v. 5) Could the servant then bring Isaac to her home? But that was not a possibility in this expedition (v. 6). The promise of God had long ago taken Abraham from his Mesopotamian roots and called him to Canaan where the Lord had said he would give that land to this patriarch (v. 7), so "if the woman will not come, you [Eliezer] are free of my oath" (v. 8). With all that understood, the servant put his hand under the thigh of Abraham, as he took the oath (v. 9). But Abraham was already sure that none of those contingencies that worried the servant would be necessary, for God had already sworn to Abraham that he would fulfill his plans promised him, therefore the servant could also be just as sure as when he too had taken the oath before Abraham (v. 7).

The Servant Meets Rebekah – 24:10–27

Eliezer packed on ten camels all sorts of gifts from his master and then set off for the place known as Aram Naharaim, meaning "Syria of the Two Rivers," where the city of Nahor was located on the Balikh River. Some think the two rivers intended here were the Euphrates and the Tigris, but instead the two were no doubt the "Habor River" and the "Balikh River." The city of Nahor may be one named Nahuru, also known to us from the Mari Texts, situated east of the Balikh River, or a city in which Abraham's brother Nahor lived. The journey must have taken something like a month to complete. Thus, the servant left the Negev, no doubt from Beersheba in 24:10, and nothing is recounted about the journey until in 24:11 when we suddenly find the servant halting the caravan at the outskirts of Nahor—all without a GPS! Was not God's angel indeed directing him over those many miles?

Eliezer arrived in the spring in Nahor in the early evening, just as the townswomen were coming out to draw water. The time these women arrived is a very different hour from the time Yeshua met the Samaritan woman who had come at noon time to draw water, presumably to avoid the reproach from the other women who knew of her questionable reputation (John 4). She came at the "sixth hour" (John 4:6–7), when none of the other women would have been there. They knew she had been remarried time and again, and that the man whom she now lived with was not her husband. She needed more than the water from that well, she needed the "living water" that only Yeshua could give to her—himself!

The servant must have prayed earnestly while he was en route, however, the text did not comment on that fact. Nevertheless, when he got to the outskirts of Nahor, he certainly prayed then:

> LORD, God of my master Abraham, make me successful today and show kindness to my master Abraham. See, I am standing beside this spring, and the daughters of the townspeople are coming out to draw water. May

it be when I say to a girl, 'Please let down your jar that I may drink,' and she says, 'Drink, and I'll water your camels too—let her be the one you have chosen for your servant Isaac. By this I will know that you have shown kindness to my master. (12–14)

It was most appropriate for this senior servant to pray for divine guidance, for how else would he have been able to determine who he should choose? Our Lord's ear is always open to the cry of his people. Even though this was in the day of the Old Testament, notice how free and unassuming this servant was about his prayer life. He did not spread a series of cloths on the ground, face east, or light a series of candles; he just spoke in his heart as if God were right there beside him, listening to his prayer. Amazing!

Even more dramatic were these words: "Before he had finished praying, Rebekah came out [of the spring or well] with her jar on her shoulder" (v. 15). The prophet Isaiah had promised: "Before they call I will answer; while they are still speaking I will hear" (65:24). That certainly was the situation in this case as well.

It turned out that this gal was the daughter of Bethuel, son of Milkah, who was the wife of Abraham's brother Nahor (v. 15). She was one beautiful girl and she also was unmarried. So, just as she promised, she went down into the spring and filled her jar. The text does not say how many times she had to go back and forth to assuage those beasts' thirst, but ten camels on the road for a month might consume up to 530 total gallons of water.[2] Imagine how many trips she had to make to fulfill her promise!

So Rebekah went "down into the well" (v. 16). It seems this well had a descending stair. Wells with these sort of stairs were not that common in the Levant, so this may have been a reservoir for rainwater. First, she gave the senior servant the promised water as she said, "Drink, my lord," an address of politeness and civility (v. 18), as she lowered the jar to her hands from her shoulder (v. 15). Often women of the East carried their jars on their heads, but Rebekah carried hers instead on her shoulders.

Then she fulfilled her promise by continuing to draw more water and emptying it into the trough (vv. 19–20). Did she act as a free agent, or was she impelled by the controlling power of God to carry out this task? Did the other servants with Eliezer join in and help in in this arduous task—of this we hear nothing in the text, so we cannot say! What we do learn is that Eliezer watched closely the diligence with which Rebekah went about her task—so much so that he was just plain amazed (vv. 20–21). The trough into which she emptied her jar time after time was probably some sort of leather trough, i.e., a simple skin set up at this well for just such a purpose.

When the camels had finished guzzling down the water, Eliezer took out a gold nose-ring, which weighed about a beka, and two gold bracelets weighing ten shekels to show her. Then he inquired whose daughter she was and whether there would be room enough for all of that traveling caravan to spend the night in their living quarters? (vv. 22–23) To this request she answered, "We have plenty of straw and fodder as well as room for you to spend the night" (v. 25). Hay was not available, so the provision for the camels would have been cut-straw mixed perhaps with barley and beans. Most would have thought that the straw was for litter on the floor, but dried dung pounded down would have been used for that purpose.

So pleased was the servant with how God had prepared the way before him that he bowed his head and worshiped God, perhaps as Rebekah was running to tell the family that a friend had arrived from far away. We are even told the content of the servant's prayer in verse 48, i.e., that while he was journeying to Aram Naharaim, the Lord had led him all that way! If this was the spiritual level to which a domestic in Abraham's household had achieved, then Abraham himself must never have taken a step unless he had first taken the matter to God in prayer. The servant continued in his prayer:

> Praise be to the LORD, the God of my master Abraham, who has not abandoned his kindness and faithfulness to my master. As for me, the LORD has led me on the journey to the house of my master's relatives. (27)

In the meantime, Rebekah had run off to her mother's tent, for the residences of the women were separate from those of the men (v. 28). Rebekah also told her bother Laban all that had happened, so off he went to meet this stranger who was still standing at the well (v. 29). However, when he saw the earrings and the bracelets on his sister's hands, his behavior toward this relative was immediately greatly influenced for the good, which, in light of the gifts, turned out to be, of course, generous (v. 30). From the subsequent narrative about Laban, we find him usually otherwise-motivated. He tended to be mercenary and could be quite affected by the display of wealth.

All this time the servant was modestly remaining at the well waiting for an official invitation to come to the tents of Rebekah's family. Laban gave that invitation in verse 31, "Come [in], you who are blessed by the LORD.

Why are you standing out here?" So, the man entered the tent of the family, as Laban, no doubt, loosened the gear that was on the camels (v. 32). Laban provided the feed for the camels and the water for the men to wash their feet.

The meal was then set before the visiting party, but the servant declined to immediately begin eating, for he felt he must discharge his mission first. In that act, we see once again the depth of the character of this senior servant of Abraham, who judged his work and commission from Abraham of more importance than his food! Regardless of whether the food was getting cold or not, Eliezer launched into his speech (verses 34–49).

Eliezer explained how Abraham had been overwhelmingly blessed by God as he had made him "great," and had given him "flocks, herds, silver, gold, men-servants, maid-servants, camels and donkeys (v. 35). God had also given to Abraham's wife a son even when the two of them were old (v. 36). So God had been uniquely good to his master, so that is why he made him swear he would not take a wife from among the Canaanites, but one from his own kindred and from his father's house for the son God had given to them (v. 27–28). Eliezer had also asked what he should do in the eventuality that this bride-to-be would not come back with him, or her family would not release her (v. 39). Abraham had responded that the Lord before whom he walked would send his angel ahead of Eliezer and would therefore prosper his task of taking a wife for his son from Abraham's kinfolks (v. 40). However, if the servant's venture failed because either the woman or the family disallowed it, he would be free from the oath.

Eliezer went on to tell how Rebekah came to the well as he was standing there with his ten camels praying that God would grant him a sign as to who he should choose for a wife for Isaac. Rebekah arrived before he had finished praying and on her own accord offered to do exactly what he had just asked God to help him with (vv. 42–47)! She proceeded to give Eliezer drink and then did the same for his camels! Eliezer concluded his speech in verse 49 by requesting that this family would deal with him kindly and truly and grant permission for Rebekah to leave with him for her wedding! Had not the Lord truly led him in the right way?

Her brother Laban and her father Bethuel answered by observing, "This is from the LORD; we can say nothing to you one way or the other," meaning it was clear the Lord had worked all these things out, so there was nothing anyone could say one way or the other; it had the blessing of God over the whole situation (v. 50)! So the permission to take Rebekah was granted.

When Abraham's servant heard this good news, he again worshiped the Lord, bowing onto the ground. Then he broke out the gifts: jewels of silver, jewels of gold, and clothes, which he gave to Rebekah, to her brother Laban, and to her mother (v. 53). Then the delayed meal followed and Eliezer and the men with him finally bedded down for the night (v. 54a).

The next morning, they all got up and the servant asked to be sent on their way (v. 54b). But Rebekah's brother and mother wanted the visiting party to stall for ten days and then she could go (v. 55). But the servant was insistent they leave immediately, seeing how God had blessed and prospered their journey so far (v. 56). They decided to ask Rebekah if she would go with them right away. Her response was clear: "I will go" (v. 58). So they sent off Rebekah and her nurse Deborah with her servant and his men (v. 59). The family blessed Rebekah as they said:

> Our sister, may you increase to thousands upon thousands;
> May your offspring possess the cities of their enemies. (60)

Rebekah and her attendants mounted their camels, and together they began their trip back to Canaan with the servant (v. 61).

Isaac, now living in the desert region of the Negev, by the well of Beer Lahai Roi, had gone out into the field one evening to meditate. When he happened to have looked up, he saw camels approaching (vv. 62–63). About the same time, Rebekah had also looked up and saw this man out in the field. She lit off her camel and asked the servant, "who was that man out in the field coming to meet them?" (v. 64) Eliezer answered, "He is my master." So, Rebekah took her veil and covered herself.

The servant reported to Isaac all that had transpired in his journey to secure a wife. Isaac took Rebekah and brought her into the tent of his mother Sarah, and he loved her and was comforted after his mother's death (v. 67).

Conclusions

1. God blessed and prospered not only the possessions of Abraham, but also the process of the search of his servant Eliezer for a wife for his son Isaac.
2. It may seem a trivial matter to devote one very long chapter to a search for a bride for Isaac, but nothing in this world is a matter of trivia with our Lord. He is an all-seeing and all-knowing God.

3. The confession of the senior servant was that by means of his numerous prayers as he journeyed along, God was with him in every step of his way and that God led him in all that he undertook.

4. The winsome heart and willing hands of Rebekah made her an ideal wife for Isaac.

Questions for Thought or Discussion

1. Why was it so important that this story be narrated in all its detail? Where was its spiritual aspect and significance to be seen?

2. Do angels still play an important role in our lives? In what ways? How can we know if an angel is present or not?

3. If "meditation" is a kind of spiritual exercise, what types of activities might be involved in such meditation?

4. Eliezer seems to have almost the same kind of access into the presence of God in prayer as believers do in our day. What differences, if any, do you see between conversational prayer in Abraham's day and how does that match up with how we today can also gain from God spiritual direction?

Lesson 13

The End of the Abrahamic Cycle

Genesis 25:1–18

"Abraham took another wife, whose name was Keturah." – Genesis 25:1

Keturah is only mentioned this one time in Genesis. Here she is called the "wife" of Abraham, but in 1 Chronicles 1:32, the text calls her "Abraham's concubine." This is very similar to the situation with Bilhah, who is identified in Genesis both as Jacob's "wife" (30:4) and as his "concubine" (35:22). On the other hand, Zilpah is also called Jacob's "wife" but never his "concubine." Moreover, if the plural form "concubines" in Genesis 25:6 was meant to include all the children of Abraham, both those of Hagar and Keturah, then both Hagar (16:3) and Keturah (25:1) are called a "wife" in one place in the text, but as "concubines" in another part of the text (25:6).

But where then is the emphasis placed within this text? If it is emphasizing that Keturah was his "wife," then this suggests Abraham married her after Sarah's death. But if the emphasis is on the fact that Keturah was his "concubine" (which implies Keturah took her place as a "secondary wife" or "mistress"), then that suggests that Abraham married her while Sarah might still be living, and the verb therefore would need to be translated as "had married" or "had taken another wife" (25:1). Moreover, that Abraham sent away Keturah's sons after he had given to each of them gifts in lieu of an inheritance might suggest that they were by now grown men.

But it is still possible that Abraham, after Sarah's death, took one of his slave girls as a "wife" to meet his need for companionship and love. The main problem most have with Keturah bearing six children after Abraham was somewhere near the age of 150 years old would be that he by now had grown too old to have children. After all, God is just as able to perform a miracle when Abraham was 150 as he was when he was 100! Remember, Abraham lived 35 years[1] after Sarah's death, so there surely was time!

The descendants of Abraham by Keturah cannot all be identified, but we are able to identify the "Midianites," who lived in the Sinaitic Peninsula, between the two arms of the Red Sea and the Gulf of Aqaba. Shuah seems to be connected to one of Job's friends, Bildad the Shuhite (Job 2:11).

However, we must note that the same name sometimes appears in two different tribes or territories. Accordingly, Genesis 10 places some of these names as descendants of Ham, while in this list with Abraham they are listed as offspring of the Semitic line. For example, the name "Sheba" appears in two different lists. In Genesis 10:7 he is a descendant of Ham, but in verse 28 he is listed as Heber's son, Joktan, while Abraham is listed as a descendant of Heber's other son, Peleg (Genesis 11:16–26)!

Abraham Distributes His Wealth – 25:5–11

Abraham left everything he owned to Isaac (25:5), but while he was still living he saw to it that the sons of his concubine each received a gift (25:6). In order to protect his empire, he gave this distribution to the concubine's children so that fights after his demise would be lessened or obviated. But the sons of Keturah are called "the sons of the concubines" (v. 6), yet did the writer used the plural "concubines" when talking only about Keturah. In Hebrew, the plural form of a noun is used when two words are closely related even if only one is plural. Here there was only one concubine, but joined to the plural "sons," hence in Hebrew it means "concubine-sons" (v. 6).

We are told that Abraham lived a 175 years and then he "breathed his last and died at a good old age" (v. 8). Then he was, as the patriarchs loved to express it, "gathered to his people" (v. 8b). This expression is used ten times in the *Torah*/Pentateuch.[2] Since this note on his death involves a fourfold process: (1) he breathes his last; (2) he dies; (3) he is gathered to his kin, and (4) he is buried, it seems significant to note that he is gathered to his kin before he is buried. If being gathered to one's kinfolks precedes being buried, then being gathered to one's kin cannot mean being entombed. It implies a belief that the deceased had a continued existence by being joined to their ancestors, whether in the netherworld or in the alternative place of the redeemed. There are six individuals of whom this phrase "gathered to his people/kin" appears in the Pentateuch. It is used of Abraham (25:8), Ishmael (25;17), Isaac (35:29); Jacob (49:29, 33); Moses (Numbers 27:13; Deuteronomy 32:50); and Aaron (Numbers 20:24; Deuteronomy 32:50). Even more interesting, four of them were not buried in an ancestral grave: Abraham, Ishmael, Moses and Aaron.

Isaac and Ishmael buried their father Abraham in the Machpelah Cave near Sarah's grave (25:9); the field of Machpelah is near Mamre. This is the same cave Abraham previously purchased from Ephron the Hittite (Genesis

23) as a burial place for Sarah. The fact that the two brothers were together at the funeral either shows that they buried the hatchet at this event, or that the two, who may have been at odds with each other, had a real or even a temporary reunion at the death of their father, just as Jacob and Esau seemed to have come together at their father's funeral (35:29).

The Abrahamic narrative comes to a close in 25:11 as God passed the blessing he had bestowed on Abraham on to his son Isaac. The only difference between Abraham's blessing and that of Isaac is that Abraham had to wait until the end of his life for the evidence of the blessing of God, whereas Isaac received that blessing as his father passed on to his reward.

Isaac settled down near Beer-lahoi-roi (v. 11b), which is where the messenger of the Lord appeared to a very-distraught and pregnant Hagar, and where subsequently Ishmael was born. Thus, the venerable pilgrim Abraham, the father of the faithful, finally finished his course of living. His life had been checkered both with trials and blessing, some to an extraordinary degree! He had been blessed by God in a most unusual way with a remarkable amount of worldly prosperity. But most significant of all was the divine decree that Abraham was "the friend of God."

Conclusions

1. Abraham married Keturah as his second wife, but a wife who was also known as his concubine.
2. Abraham is not only the father of the Hebrew people, but of the Arab peoples that came from his Egyptian wife, Hagar, and his son Ishmael.
3. Isaac was the recipient of the law of primogenitor whereby he received the estate of Abraham, even though gifts were given out to the sons of Keturah before Abraham died.

Questions for Thought or Discussion

1. In retrospect, is the conflict between Ishmael and Isaac reflected in the Arab-Israeli conflicts through the ages, even today?
2. Was Abraham's marriage to Keturah also a mistake which has produced similar world problems?
3. Is the expression "gathered to his kin/people" an Old Testament way of announcing that godly believers in the Old Testament were at death immediately joined with their loved ones who had gone before?

Endnotes

Preface

1. I am indebted to one my students and subsequent colleagues, Professor Duane Garrett, for this title and the key ideas of this Preface in his book *Rethinking Genesis: The Sources and Authorship of the First Book of the Pentateuch* (Grand Rapids: Baker Book House, 1991), 159–168.

2. I am indebted to Duane Garrett, *Rethinking Genesis: The Sources and Authorship of the First Book or the Pentateuch* (Grand Rapids: Baker, 1991), 121–25, for the general idea of this outline for Genesis.

3. Of the thirteen references, Genesis 10:32 and 25:13 were regarded as repetitious and thus did not mark off separate tablets. P. J. Wiseman (the father of Donald J. Wiseman), *Ancient Records and the Structure of Genesis*, later reprinted as *Clues to Creation in Genesis*, ed. D. J. Wiseman (London: Marshall, Morgan & Scott, 1977), 3–105, and R. K. Harrison, *Introduction to the Old Testament* (Grand Rapids: Eerdmans, 1969), 543–53.

Lesson 1

1. F. B. Meyer, *Abraham: Friend of God* (Fort Washington, PA: Christian Literature Crusade, 1968), 13.

2. C. Westermann, *The Promises to the Fathers* (Philadelphia: Fortress Press, 1980), 146–47.

3. J. J. Bimson, *Redating the Exodus and Conquest* (Sheffield: JSOT Press, 1978), 219–25.

Lesson 2

1. John H. Sailhamer, "Exodus," in *The Expositor's Bible Commentary, Vol. 1, Revised Edition*, eds. Tremper Longman III and David E. Garland (Grand Rapids: Zondervan, 2008), 158–160.

2. Ibid.

3. See J. J. Davis, "The Camel in Biblical Narratives," in *A Tribute to Gleason Archer*, ed. W. C. Kaiser, Jr., and R. F. Youngblood (Chicago: Moody, 1986), 143–52.

Lesson 3

1. Meyer, *Abraham*, 40.

Lesson 4

1. The names of the four kings from Mesopotamia have the ring of authenticity. For example, Kedorlamer of Elam is certainly an Elamite name, for it has the a common *kudur* ("servant") element followed by the name of their god. Arioch of Ellasar exhibits a similar name Arriyuk(ki), which is attested in both Mari and Nuzi as a Hurrian name, even though Ellasar, the name of his kingdom, still has not been identified. Tidal of Goiim, or "nations/Gentiles," is equivalent to the name of four Hittite kings named Tudhaliya. His kingdom may relate to a similar term applied to first-millennium Cimmerians and then to the Medes. The name Amraphel has been (unsuccessfully) linked to Hammurabi. His kingdom of Shinar, however, denotes Babylon. See Kenneth Kitchen, "The Patriarchal Age: Myth or History?" *BAR* 21, 56–57.

2. T. O. Lambdin, "Egyptian Loan Words in the Old Testament," *JAOS* 73 (1953), 150.

Lesson 5

1. Hebrew "Eliezer" in an apocopated form in Greek becomes *Lazaros*, or in English "Lazarus" in Luke 16:23. The rich man and Lazarus represents Lazarus in "Abraham's bosom," which might be a covert allusion to the fact that here was another Gentile who had been converted and put his faith in the coming "Man of Promise."

2. The Nuzi Tablets were discovered in 1925 near Kirkuk, a branch of the Tigris River. They date from the fifteenth century B.C.E. The people of Nuzi seem to be non-Semitic Hurrians, i.e., the Horites of the Bible. It is thought they reflect the fact that customs lingered on for years.

3. T. V. Farris, *Mighty to Save: A Study in Old Testament Soteriology* (Nashville: Broadman, 1993), 76–77. Emphasis added.

4. Allen P. Ross, "The Biblical Method of Salvation: A Case of Discontinuity," in *Continuity and Discontinuity*, ed. John Feinberg (Westchester, IL: Crossway, 1988), 168. Emphasis added.

5. For the most comprehensive discussion of this event, see Gerhard F. Hasel, "The Meaning of the Animal Rite in Genesis 15," *Journal for the Study of the Old Testament* 19 (1981): 61–78. Also see the response of G. J. Wenham, "The Symbolism of the Animal Rite in Genesis 15:7, *JSOT* 22 (1982): 134–37.

Lesson 6

1. Additional references to the "Angel of the LORD" appear in Judges 13:3; 15–18, 20, 21; 1 Kings 19:5; 2 Chronicles 32:21; Psalm 8:5; 91:11; 103:20; 104:4; 148:2; Daniel 3:28; 6:22; Matthew 4:11; 13:41; 25:31; Luke 2:13, 15; Hebrews 1:4ff.

2. So argued John H. Sailhamer in "Genesis," *The Expositor's Bible Commentary*, 179.

3. See for example Ronald Youngblood, *Faith of Our Fathers: A Bible Commentary for Laymen* (Glendale, CA, Regal Books: 1976), 37.

4. John Sailhamer, "Genesis," 182.

Lesson 7

1. It should also be noted that the Hebrew scribes called the Masoretes marked this verse as "holy." Several manuscripts read the name "Yahweh" in place of *ADONAI*.

2. Victor P. Hamilton, *pele'* in *The Theological Wordbook of the Old Testament, Vol. II*, eds. R. Laird Harris, Gleason L. Archer, Jr., and Bruce K. Waltke (Chicago: Moody Press, 1980), 723.

3. As suggested by Sailhamer, "Genesis," 191.

4. For more detail, see Walter C. Kaiser, Jr., "The Prayer of Abraham for a Wicked City," in *I Will Lift My Eyes Unto the Hills: Learning From the Great Prayers of the Old Testament* (Bellingham, WA: Lexham Press, 2015), 7–17.

5. The eighteen texts containing the "emendations of the scribes" are: Genesis 18:22; Numbers 11:15, 12:12; 1 Samuel 3:13; 2 Samuel 16:12, 20:1; 1 Kings 12:16; 2 Chronicles 10:16; Jeremiah 2:11; Ezekiel 8:17; Hosea 4:7; Habakkuk 1:12; Zechariah 2:12 [Eng. 8]; Malachi 1:12; Psalm 106:20; Job 7:20, 32:3; Lamentations 3:20. The reason the scribes changed these texts, but left a note in the margin as to what they had done, was to avoid what they thought was irreverent, idolatrous, or blasphemous expressions.

Lesson 8

1. For further information, see Walter C. Kaiser, Jr., "Homosexuality: Romans 1:24–27," in *What Does the Lord Require? A Guide for Preaching and Teaching Biblical Ethics* (Grand Rapids: Baker Academic, 2009), 117–26.

2. For an interesting article, see Amos Frumkin, "How Lot's Wife Became a Pillar of Salt," *BAR* 35 (May/June 2009): 38–44.

3. Not all agree with this identification. For example Stephen Collins does not in his article "Where Is Sodom? The Case for Tall el-Hammam," in *BAR* 39 (March/April 2013): 32–41. He places the

Cities of the Plain about 14 miles northeast of the Dead Sea in a large oval-shaped fertile plain called *ha-kikkar*, meaning "the disc" (Genesis 13:13).

4. Bryant Wood, "The Discovery of the Sin Cities of Sodom and Gomorrah," *Bible and Spade* 16 (2008).

Lesson 9

1. Meyer, *Abraham*, 115.

2. Ibid., 112.

3. Clark H. Pinnock, "Conscience," in *Baker's Dictionary of Christian Ethics*, ed. Carl F. H. Henry (Grand Rapids: Baker Book House, 1973), 126–27.

4. Ibid., 127.

Lesson 10

1. Søren Kierkegaard. *Fear and Trembling*, 1843; trans. H. V. Hong and E. H. Hong (Princeton: Princeton University, 1983).

Lesson 11

1. During the Patriarchal period, the "shekel" was not a coin; it was a weight. Coinage came much later, in the 700s B.C.E.

2. See the article by M. R. Lehmann, "Abraham's Purchase of Machpelah and Hittite Law," *BASOR* 129 (February 1953): 15–18. The two Hittite laws from the Hittite Law Code were laws 46 and 47. See the translation of these two laws in A. Goetze, *ANET*, 191.

Lesson 12

1. See R. D. Freedman, "'Put Your Hand Under My Thigh' – The Patriarchal Oath," *BAR* 2/2 (1976): 3–4, 42.

2. Usually a camel can drink about 26 to 40 gallons of water at one stop, but if they had not stopped to water the camels in about one month, then they had a capacity of 53 gallons each, which they could digest in three minutes.

Lesson 13

1. Sarah lived to be 127 years old (Genesis 23:1), thus there were some 36 or 37 years after the birth of Isaac (17:1, 21:5).

2. See Genesis 25:8, 17; 35:29; 49:29, 33; Numbers 20:24, 26; 27:13; 31:2; Deuteronomy 32:50. There is a related phrase, "He was gathered to [or buried with] his fathers" in Genesis 15:15, 47:30 and elsewhere in the Old Testament, e.g., Judges 2:10.

Printed in the United States
by Baker & Taylor Publisher Services